Stoicism: Cobwebs and Gems

AN INFORMAL CONVERSATION
BETWEEN TWO MODERN STOICS

Dr. Chuck Chakrapani & Tim LeBon

The Stoic Gym Publications
www.TheStoicGym.com

www.TheStoicGym.com

Chuck Chakrapani & Tim LeBon
Stoicism: Cobwebs and Gems - —1st ed
Chuck Chakrapani & Tim LeBon.
ISBN
978-0-920219-82-9 Paperback
978-0-920219-83-6 epub

Contents

Introduction by Tim LeBon 7

STOICISM IN THE MODERN AGE

1. Setting the Stage 11

2. The Importance of Clearing the Cobwebs 19

3. Non-rational Beliefs 21

4. Starting with the SABS Scale 29

STOIC ATTITUDE AND BEHAVIOUR SCALE

5. Is the Universe Benevolent? 33

6. Is the Universe a Living Thing? 41

7. Does the Universe Embody Wisdom? 51

8. Does the Universe Embody Wisdom? [2] 61

9. Does an agnostic behave like an atheist? 69

STOIC PHYSICS, GOD, AND DETERMINISM

10. Did the Ancient Stoics Believe in God? 71

11. Is Stoic Physics the Foundation or a Pedestal?. 83

12. How about Epicureanism? 115

13. Did the Ancient Stoics *Truly* Believe in God?.. 121

14. Can Compatibilism Save Stoic Determinism?. 129

15. Final Thoughts 141

During the Fall-Winter 2020 season, two modern Stoics, Tim LeBon and Dr. Chuck Chakrapani, exchanged a series of letters on modern Stoicism though letter.wiki. *This is the edited and modified version of their conversations with additional references.*

Tim LeBon is an accredited CBT psychotherapist, counsellor, and Stoic Life Coach in private practice in London (UK) and one of the founders of Modern Stoicism.

Dr. Chuck Chakrapani is the editor of THE STOIC *magazine and the author of more than fifteen books on Stoicism.*

Stoic Ethics is ultimately parasitical on physics.
A.A. LONG[1]

We find no texts in which virtue, impulse and the like are derived from Stoic physics. [...] We have no support for the claim that Stoic ethics can only be understood in terms of the concepts of Stoic physics.

JULIA ANNAS[2]

Introduction by Tim LeBon

I was delighted to be invited by Peter Limburg of the Toronto Stoics to take part in an exchange of letters on Stoicism to be published live on the internet. I had previously enjoyed dialogues with others in the Modern Stoicism movement, especially Chris Gill. The opportunity to correspond with Chuck excited me. I first met Chuck in Toronto in a hotel lobby during Stoicon 2017. Like a modern-day Socrates, Chuck interrogated me about the nature of Stoicism. "What do you think are the elements we really need in Stoicism?" he asked. I think I mumbled something about the dichotomy of control and virtue. He nodded. When I added something about other aspects of Stoicism being interesting but perhaps not essential, Chuck looked more skeptical. These letters have provided the opportunity for us to extend that conversation.

Why should you take any interest in our conversation? For one thing, you might find yourself nodding in agreement with Bertie Wooster's opinion expressed in P.G. Wodehouse's classic of comic writing, *The Mating Season*.

Jeeves said, "I wonder if I might draw your attention to an observation of the Emperor Marcus Aurelius? He said, 'Does anything befall you? It is good. It is part of the destiny of the universe ordained for you from the beginning. All that befalls you is part of the great web."'

I breathed a bit stertorously. "He said that, did he?"

"Yes, sir."

"'Well, you can tell him from me he's an ass."

Whilst you might not go so far as to call Marcus Aurelius or Seneca an ass like Bertie Wooster, do you begin to have doubts when they talk of fate, God, Providence, or Pantheism? Have you ever thought, "If this is an essential part of Stoicism – include me out!" So, it's important to explore whether these really are essential parts of Stoicism.

In my work as a therapist, coach, and trainer, I hope to convey ideas in an economical, convincing, and helpful manner. Why teach people five complicated ideas when they can benefit as much by learning three simple and less controversial ideas? We should consider the possibility that Chuck's minimalism may be more economical and convincing than traditional alternatives.

As you will see, Chuck and I do not always agree on all the details. Some traditional Stoics, old and new, would disagree more. Why should our views be of any relevance? I am not an academic philosopher or classicist, but I have trained as a philosopher and philosophical counselor and have attempted to *live* informed by philosophical ideas for many years. I am both a self-declared *prokopton* (making progress) and no Stoic sage. I hope that our conversation both entertains and helps the reader on their own path towards wisdom and virtue.

Tim LeBon
Guildford, United Kingdom
February 2021

Setting the Stage

LETTER 1. CHUCK TO TIM

 Let's start with an important issue: clearing the 'cobwebs' around Stoicism. We all know how relevant Stoicism is for the digital age. Yet there are aspects of Stoicism which may be archaic. To begin the discussion, here is my understanding of what Stoicism is.

WHAT IS STOICISM? [3] [4]

We fret about things we can do nothing about and fail to act on what is under our control. Most of our unhappiness comes from the fact that we try to control what is not under our control and fail to act on what *is* under our control. In other words, we judge our 'impressions' incorrectly.

Stoicism says that the first thing we need to be clear about is that some things in our lives are up to us, and others are not. Things that are up to us are what we believe, what we desire or hate, and what we move toward or avoid. Almost all other things are not in our control. We can avoid a lot of trouble and achieve happiness by ignoring what we have no control over and acting on what we *do* have control over.

The reason we act this way and make ourselves unhappy is that we often act irrationally; we don't live a 'life according to Nature'. Nature means our nature (which is rationality) and according to the nature of the world (which is the way things are). So, we must act rationally and not struggle against reality.

We can achieve this, by using four special skills:

- *Wisdom* (resourcefulness and discretion)

- *Justice* (understanding that we are part of society)

- *Courage* (not being afraid of things we don't control such as sickness and poverty)

- *Moderation* (avoiding excess)

A person who lives rationally would be wise, just, courageous, and moderate. The Stoics called these four special skills virtues. Using these four skills is fundamental to Stoicism.

We can achieve total happiness by acting on what is under our control. But what about all those other things that are not under our control? A wonderful house, a shiny new car, or super health? They may be good to have but whatever is not under our total control is not necessary for our happiness. You can be happy with or without them. It is natural to prefer wealth to poverty, health to sickness. But should we lose them, we can still be happy.

Stoics are not ascetics. They say that we are free to enjoy 'desirable' things such as health and wealth as long as we remember that they are not under our control and we do not use them to harm ourselves or others. Think of all the great things you have as things on loan to you that can be called back at any time. As long as they are not called back, you are free to enjoy them any way you like.

Life is a festival. We should enjoy whatever life offers us but shouldn't chase after things.

Although I consider the above as the essence of Stoicism, strictly speaking, it is an outline of 'Stoic ethics'. (Ethics is that part of Stoicism concerned with 'virtue, happiness, impulse, appropriation, and the rest of these ideas'.)[5] Ancient Stoics considered Stoic ethics as only one part of Stoicism, the other parts being logic and physics. We can set aside logic for the time being because we need logic to learn *any* subject, not just Stoicism. The question is whether we need Stoic physics at all to understand and practice Stoicism.

There are many modern Stoics, including some highly distinguished Stoic scholars such as Chris Gill, Brad Inwood, A.A. Long, and others who believe that Stoic physics is an essential or a desirable component of Stoicism and Stoicism needs Stoic physics to work.

I neither claim to be a Stoic scholar nor do I feel that I have the intellectual heft to be one. So, what are my credentials? Just this: I see myself as an ordinary citizen, a non-philosopher passing by the ancient agora. I stand by the *stoa poikile*, listening attentively to the Stoics. I am not concerned about defining every word precisely or getting into an academic discussion of what the Stoic *would* or *could* have meant. I am concerned only about getting the major concepts right, so my life will work better. What I hear convinces me that Stoicism is open to anyone who spends time understanding it, even though they may not possess any academic credentials, and even though they couldn't compare what Spinoza said with what Stoics said.

When I talk with (or read the writings of) Stoic scholars such as Chris Gill, Brad Inwood, or A.A. Long, I find a great deal of inclusivity in the way they view Stoicism. And yet, I don't see the same tolerance among many other academics and practitioners. For example, in my early days of joining the Stoic online communities, whenever I expressed a contrary view in a Stoic Facebook group, many of the community members would label me as being ignorant. It is possible that my views were ignorant, but the swift and ferocious comments I received did not convince me of that.

Dogmatic views will likely lead us astray

Any dogmatic view of what Stoicism is will likely lead us away from Stoicism. Of course, I am not suggesting that Stoicism is a free-for-all, and it is whatever you say it is. What I am saying is that when a serious non-traditional view is expressed, we should be prepared to examine *the reasons that led up to the view* rather than attempting to discredit the view itself with alternative arguments (as happened to my own 2018 article, *Stoic Minimalism*,[6] when all refutations were of my *views* and not refutations of the *reasons* that led up to my views[7]) or dismiss it entirely, as happened elsewhere.[8]

Scarcity of first-hand accounts of Stoicism

Why is this important? Because we have no proper first-hand record of Stoicism as a philosophy and we need to get as close to 'true' Stoic thought as we reasonably can. Stoic philosophy was developed over a period of 500 years and yet this is all we have to go by:

1. Records of early Stoic thought by Cicero,[9] who was not even born when the last scholarch of early Stoicism died.

2. Records (mostly anecdotal) of Stoic philosophers and their thoughts by Diogenes Laërtius,[10] who was barely born when the last great Stoic, Marcus Aurelius, died.

3. Extensive works of Seneca[11] whose work is mostly the application of Stoic principles. (Seneca's writings are not generally considered canonical.)

4. First-hand records of some of Epictetus' teachings by his student Flavius Arrian.[12] (These are likely to be Epictetus' conversations with his students and visitors rather than formal lecture notes.)

5. Personal reflections[13] of the Stoic emperor, Marcus Aurelius, in battlefields.

6. Fragments and non-contemporaneous anthologies of Stoic teachings by different ancient Stoics such as the one collected by Stobaeus[14] who probably lived around the fifth century, CE.

7. The works of the Platonist Plutarch, the Pyrrhonist Sceptic Sextus Empiricus, and the physician Galen.

That is pretty much it. These sources are either non-systematic first-hand exposition or second-hand summaries of Stoicism. The fact that we don't have any systematic first-hand account makes room for several self-appointed authorities on the subject.

The difficulty in distinguishing essentials from the irrelevant and the incidental

If we have no systematic first-hand account of Stoicism, then it is difficult to distinguish essential Stoic thoughts from incidental and even irrelevant ones. Let me give you a couple of examples.

- Musonius Rufus gives detailed arguments for vegetarianism.[15] As he was a prominent Stoic and, if his was the only Stoic work that survived, then we would probably consider vegetarianism as an essential part of Stoicism. But we know from other sources (such as Epictetus[16] and Marcus Aurelius[17]) that this is not so.

- Seneca says in his *The Firmness of the Wiseman:*

  There is as wide a difference between the Stoics and the other sects of philosophers as there is between men and women ...the one is born to command, the other to obey.

  Yet there are passages in the writings of Epictetus[18] and Musonius Rufus[19] that would lead us to believe that Stoicism itself is not sexist, given the cultural context of ancient times. The sexist language sometimes found in Stoic writings such as the one cited above is more likely to be the result of the ancient Stoics using the idiom of their days and not their considered view on the subject. At no place in Stoic writings do we find evidence that Stoicism as a philosophy considers women inferior to men.

What I am trying to say is, when there is no systematic but only a relatively sparse record of what Stoicism is, it is difficult to distinguish what some Stoics might have taught or said from what Stoicism is. As the above examples show, *we cannot assume that everything the Stoics taught is necessarily Stoicism.* Therefore, the proposition I would like to explore is this,

> *Not all of what ancient Stoics taught can be interpreted as Stoic philosophy.*

It might be worthwhile sorting out what the essential teachings of Stoicism were from the optional ones (and those not even necessarily Stoic).

I would like to propose (but am willing to stand corrected) that *the essential teachings of Stoicism are entirely contained in Stoic ethics.* All other aspects of Stoicism are ornamental and superfluous. Most prominent of all is the assumed connection between Stoic physics and Stoic ethics. I believe it is tenuous at best, non-existent at worst. What are your thoughts, Tim?

The Importance of Clearing the Cobwebs

LETTER 2. TIM TO CHUCK

 It's great to have this opportunity to talk with you. I have very much enjoyed your presentations of Stoicism in both Toronto and Athens. It's so good that you outlined your 'simplified Stoicism' here again at the start of our correspondence. I especially appreciated how you simplify Stoicism and present it in a coherent and compelling manner.

We know little about ancient Stoic practices

I also enjoyed your list of how little we know about how Stoicism was really practiced and are missing so much of the original source material. I guess that it is a call for humility when any of us (myself included) make a claim about what Stoicism really is.

I do wonder though whether it's quite as bad as you say – the scholars seem to be agreed that Cicero is a reliable source, for example. Chris Gill has cited (in an unpublished dialogue) that *On Duties* is one of the best sources of Stoic ethics. To be honest, though, although the history of Stoicism fascinates me, what interests me more is developing a workable version of something akin to ancient Stoicism, whether it would have met with the approval of Zeno or even Epictetus. That for me is the exciting potential for a Modern Stoicism.[20]

I say this because I work as a psychotherapist and life coach, and don't want to ask people to try something that isn't likely to make sense to them or help them. Nor should it be based on a worldview inconsistent with our best understanding of how things are in the twenty-first century (i.e., modern science).

The importance of identifying the cobwebs

So, getting rid of any cobweb in Stoicism is important – as long as they really are cobwebs. One person's 'cobweb' could be another's 'gem', so it's important for us to distinguish the cobwebs from the gems. One thought though. You say that it is just ethics we should be concerned with, but don't we also need Stoic psychology? For example, something like the cognitive theory of the emotions?[21] Perhaps you can spell out more.

Non-rational Beliefs

LETTER 3. CHUCK TO TIM

Thank you for your thoughts, Tim.

First let me address the concern you raised about Stoic psychology. I would consider Stoic psychology to be a part of Stoic ethics, and, if not, at least closely related to it. So, I have no issues with it. In fact, I would consider Stoic psychology as partly the foundation and partly the extension of Stoic ethics. In a broad sense, Stoic psychology can be the foundation and the purpose of Stoic ethics.

To provide some context to my letters, I am dazzled by the clarity and the Stoic scholarship of people like Chris Gill, Pierre Hadot, Brad Inwood, David Sedley, and A.A. Long, and admire critical thinkers like Larry Becker, Tad Brennan, and Julia Annas. As I said earlier, I raise the issue of Stoic cobwebs purely as a layman – not as a philosopher, not as an expert, not as an intellectual, not as a scholar. I don't claim to be any of those.

My approach to Stoicism

I approach these issues as someone who believes that Stoicism is aimed at laypeople and therefore should not be beyond their grasp. From a symbolic perspective, the ancient Stoics did not teach from the grand temple of Lyceum or retreat to a garden. They chose to stand and teach in the busiest marketplace in Athens, perhaps in the entire world, at that time. They chose to deliver their teachings from an open structure, so any passerby could listen and learn. If their philosophy could be understood only by elite interpretation, then I am sure they would have chosen a different venue for their lectures.

When I read Stoic ethics, I understand how it is in line with my own experience and how it can potentially lead to a good life. I see the logic behind Stoic ethics and notice it is not, by and large, based on any non-rational beliefs.

It all makes sense to me. Then I am told that Stoic physics (which includes what we would now call metaphysics) provides the basis for, or in any case is intertwined with, Stoic ethics,

> The foundations of Stoic ethics are to be sought...in cosmology and theology.[22]

> Stoic Ethics is ultimately parasitical on physics. [23]

Very well, then. So, I go read Stoic physics to get a better understanding of Stoic ethics. As you know, Stoic physics[24] includes natural science,[25] metaphysics,[26] and theology[27] and covers topics such as:

1. How Zeus created this world and set in motion the course of events; what is active and what is passive; what is logos?[28]
2. How inert things got life and how everything is a continuum.
3. How the universe began, was destroyed, and recreated.
4. The deterministic nature of our world and everything in it.
5. Whatever exists (including human soul), exists as a physical body.

The accompanying box briefly summarizes the principles of Stoic physics.

STOIC PHYSICS: A BRIEF OUTLINE[29]

The evolution and dissolution of the cosmos

Our world has a starting point. Before that, all that existed was the perfection of Zeus (God or Reason). Zeus or Reason was (and is) corporeal and continuous in space. Everything else was inert.

Zeus organized inert matter by pervading through it, creating the living body and the cosmos. Creation started when divine fire condensed into liquid. This liquid is partly vaporized and partly condensed into earth, while the fire continued to exist. It was the source of all objects and all changes to come. The principles inherent in fire drove the creation and development of our world.

Air, the divine breath or pneuma, enters and rules the inert matter. Air, Fire, Earth, and Water are called the four elements. Air and Fire are light elements dominated by active principles; Earth and Water are heavy elements dominated by passive principles. When we are dominated by an active principle, we are rational and divine; when dominated by a passive principle, we are less so.

The power of fire will keep increasing until one day the fuel will be exhausted and, as a result, the entire cosmos will go up in flames. Then the entire cycle will start repeating itself, over and over again. (Later Stoics such as Panaetius, the last Scholarch, as well as Posidonius rejected this view.)

The hierarchy of beings

The entire cosmos is a rational animal but there is a hierarchy. The hierarchy is determined by the nature of the pneuma[30] or the 'divine breath' that shaped the cosmos.

- God has perfect logos ('active reason that is perfect') and therefore he is on the top of the Stoic hierarchy.

- Humans come next. They have logos.

- Then come non-rational animals. They can perceive.

- Plants come fourth. They neither think nor perceive but they respond to their environment.

All non-living stuff is inert and therefore at the bottom of the hierarchy.

The world is an interaction between the active principle (fire, air, or pneuma) and the passive principle. They constitute a dynamic continuum, fluid and in flux with no independent part. There is no void in the cosmos. It begins only at the edge of the cosmos.

The human soul

The human soul consists of eight streams: five senses and three faculties (reproduction, speech, and command). All our cognition takes place in our command center. Command faculty controls the remaining seven streams of the human soul. It is a two-way street from the center to the surface and back.

The creative force

Eros, the god of Love, is the creative force. It unifies the opposites, bringing active and passive principles together. Life is created, nurtured, and reproduced though Love and it is as important as eating, resting, sleeping, and other important activities. As a rational being, one can experience love without attachment to any particular person, place, or thing.

Death, loosening of soul's tension

Death occurs when the soul loosens its tension and separates from the human body. Even though the active and passive principles are thoroughly intertwined, they retain their unique properties and separate at death. The soul then joins with the 'world soul'. In Stoic physics, there is no reward or punishment after death. There is no heaven, no hell.

Causality and determinism

The universe is causal. Seasons follow one another in the same sequence. A tree is caused by a tree, a cat is caused by a cat, and a human being is caused by a human being. Thus, the course of the universe is predetermined by a causal chain. The causal chain is unbroken and continuous through time and space. Free will is just an appearance. We may have freedom to act in any way we like, but our destination is already decided.

Unresolvable issues and non-rational beliefs

What do I make of Stoic physics? Let me put it in context.

I am not bothered personally about what people believe in: gods, demons, extraterrestrials, the Bermuda triangle, flat earth, or whatever. For me, I believe that certain issues, no matter how many people are certain that they know the answer, are unresolvable. Such issues include:

- Whether God exists or not.

- Whether life is completely predetermined or not.

- Whether free will exists or not.

I believe any system of thought that demands us to subscribe to a given set of beliefs in these matters is non-rational (but not necessarily irrational).

Given that Stoic physics takes definite positions on matters that I believe to be non-resolvable issues, I need to ask,

Does Stoic physics in any way enhance my understanding of Stoic ethics? Do I have to believe in Stoic physics as an essential prerequisite or is it just an ornamental decoration around Stoic ethics?

If it turns out that Stoic ethics cannot work without Stoic physics, then Stoicism loses its attraction for me because I am not a big fan of what I consider to be non-rational beliefs. If, on the other hand, Stoic physics really has only a tenuous bearing on Stoic ethics, then Stoic physics is not really an essential part of Stoicism. Belief in it is optional. One can connect the two if one wants to (as many people have already done) and take comfort in that. We can use the principles of Stoic ethics to better our lives. We can use them in psychological counseling and therapies as we are doing now. We can be Stoics without having to take any position on God, free will, the way the world came about, who decides what happens next, etc.

Why do I start with Stoic physics? If we want to separate the wheat from the chaff, we should probably start with the part where chaff far exceeds wheat. To me, that place seems to be Stoic physics. I don't necessarily expect you to agree with me on this now or even when I explain my reasoning behind it.

Nevertheless, if you want to continue the conversation out of intellectual curiosity, I would like to explore each of the major topics of Stoic physics with you, such as God, the origin of the universe, free will, etc., and explain why I think Stoic physics is untenable. You can accept it, reject it, suspend judgment on it, or maybe even make me change my mind!

My conclusions are my own for which I will provide rationale. They are not prescriptive, and no one needs to accept them if they're not convinced what I say makes sense. Let me know if you would like to continue.

Starting with the SABS Scale

LETTER 4. TIM TO CHUCK

Three basic issues

Thank you for your latest letter.
My first thought is that we have three questions lurking here:

1. Which parts of Stoicism are untenable? (What are the cobwebs?)

2. What is left of Stoicism once we remove the cobwebs?

3. If we remove these cobwebs, is the rest of Stoicism tenable? Or is it more like a tabletop that has lost its

support (as some writers say that the ethics is supported by the physics and logic)?

I'm interested in all these questions, and perhaps we can get around to all of them. I'm happy to start with question one, which seems to be the one of most immediate interest to you.

So, what parts of Stoicism are untenable? I don't think we can go as far as to say that *all* of the physics is obviously wrong, or that *all* of the ethics and psychology is obviously right. Some of the ethics is not *at all* intuitively self-evident.

For example, Epicureans thought that pleasure and not virtue was the main good. Even more controversial (in ancient times, and now) is the theory of preferred indifferents with which everyone else disagreed – the idea that virtue is the only thing that is *really good* but other 'external goods' such as health, wealth, and status may have value but of a qualitatively different nature to virtue. Cynics disagreed because it didn't give virtue its due place, and others including Aristotle, disagreed because it placed too little weight on values other than virtue.[31]

I mention these because if the ethics is not self-evident, we need to provide some good reasons to let it rule our lives – as opposed, for example, to rival Epicurean, Cynic, or Aristotelian views. This leads to my next two questions and the justification of an ethics and psychology-based Stoicism.

Starting with the SABS Scale

If we look at worldview and physics, maybe a good place to start is the SABS – the Stoic Attitudes and Behaviours Scale.[32] In the SABS 5.0, we have several Stoic ideas under worldview, namely:

1. The universe is benevolent in its overall plan.

2. The universe is a living thing.

3. There is no overall plan to the universe. (A reversed item, i.e., the Stoics believed that there is a plan.)

4. There is a rational and orderly plan in the universe and in the causes of events.

5. The universe embodies wisdom.

Clearly these five items overlap. They also overlap with the items you listed in your last letter, namely:

1. How Zeus created this world and set in motion the course of events; what is active and what is passive; what is logos.

2. How inert things got life and how everything is a continuum.

3. How the universe began, was destroyed, and recreated.

4. The deterministic nature of our world and everything in it.

5. Whatever exists (including the human soul), exists as a physical body.

Comparing the SABS worldview items and your list, Chuck, it looks like SABS doesn't mention certain aspects of physics that you include – such as Zeus, the beginnings of the universe or materialism (items one, two, three and five in your list). So, it could be that the 'Modern Stoics' who created SABS (Donald Robertson, Chris Gill, me, and some others) either didn't think items one, two, three and five were so central to Stoic worldview or perhaps not so justifiable as the other items. That's not to say there aren't Stoics out there who believe in the whole physics – but I think most modern Stoics would not want to include Stoic ideas about the creation and destruction of the universe, and perhaps about Zeus – but we probably will need to talk about Stoicism and God later!

I propose that we focus on the SABS items. Would you like to take up an invitation to argue against the SABS worldview items, which I think can be rephrased as:

- The universe is a living thing.
- The universe embodies wisdom.
- There is a rational and orderly plan in the universe and in the causes of events.
- The universe is benevolent in its overall plan.

What do you think?

Is the Universe Benevolent?

LETTER 5. CHUCK TO TIM

 Thank you for your crisp analysis and thoughtful questions. As I said earlier, I don't consider myself any more than a layman and I am not foolish enough to presume to know definitive answers to your questions, or even to my own. I'm thinking along certain lines and I am trying to explore their validity with you.

Test of rationality

If I ever must take anything seriously and apply it to my life, it should pass the test of rationality. Stoic ethics passes this test relatively easily. I am not so sure about Stoic physics though. So instead of pronouncing definitively what is wheat and what is chaff, what is gem and what is cobweb, and what we will find eventually, I would like to discuss those parts of ancient Stoicism that I consider untenable. As I indicated in my previous letter, "you can accept it, reject it, suspend judgment on it, or maybe even make me change my mind". With these caveats in mind, here is my response to your questions.

1. Which parts of Stoicism are untenable? (What are the cobwebs?)

I believe those parts of Stoicism that are based on a non-rational belief system, parts that contradict established science, are untenable. This is not a revolutionary or a novel idea. From Aristo of Chios to Tad Brennan, Stoic thinkers have challenged the assumptions of orthodox Stoicism. A large part of what I consider cobwebs comes from Stoic physics. Some aspects of Stoic logic and ethics may also qualify.

2. What is left of Stoicism once we remove the cobwebs?

This is what I believe will be left after the cobwebs are cleared: (a) almost the entire structure of Stoic ethics; (b) those parts of Stoic logic that correspond to what we understand by logic today – such as syllogisms, modal logic, propositional logic, etc.; and (c) some minor parts of Stoic physics.

3. If we remove these cobwebs, is the rest of Stoicism tenable or even a hidden gem? Or is it more like a tabletop that has lost its support (as some writers say that the ethics is supported by the physics and logic)?

This is an interesting and important point. I have thought about it a lot. I venture to say that what is generally assumed to be the foundation (or the legs of a table) is nothing more than a pedestal upon which Stoic ethics is placed. When we remove the cobwebs, we won't have a table without legs but a gem we can place on any pedestal.

Let me start with the point with which you began the discussion,

> *I don't think we can go as far as to say that the physics is obviously untenable, and ethics and psychology are obviously right.*

Of course, we cannot, unless we can show that Stoic physics is untenable, and ethics and psychology are. I hope this series of letters will help us to decide one way or another, if not fully, at least partially. You say that:

1. *Some aspects of Stoic ethics are not intuitive.*
2. *Stoic worldview as described by SABS has an approximate correspondence to the physical issues outlined by me.*

and suggest that SABS may be a good place to start. Well, let's do that. I would be happy to discuss the many issues you list, but one at a time. Let me start with the last SABS item on your list.

Is the universe benevolent?

The universe is benevolent in its overall plan.

The idea that the universe is benevolent has been accepted by many Stoic scholars. For example, Long and Sedley have this to say,

In Stoicism, the logos is understood to be the perfectly rational benevolent Nature of the universe.[33]

Do I want to take issue with it? It depends on the context. *There are beneficial statements that may not be true and true statements that may not be beneficial.* If I view things from a helping professional's point of view, the belief that *the universe is benevolent in its overall plan* is probably a beneficial one to most people with little downside to it. So, as a helping professional I might use it, even if I know I have no proof of it. Just as I would not consider a physician helping a hypochondriac with a placebo unethical, I would not consider a therapist using non-rational statements to alleviate the distress of a patient unethical either.

But, if you ask me whether I want to take issue with it as a rational statement, I will probably say yes, unless you can prove it to me otherwise. If you ask me why, I will probably cite Brad Inwood,

If the determined world is part of a grand plan aimed at producing the good, why is there so much bad in the world?[34]

Do the Stoics have a convincing answer? Not really. Brad Inwood again,

What do the Stoics have to say for themselves? Alas, their answers do not represent their finest work.[35]

The Stoic answers are all over the place. One answer is that God was constrained by the material he had to work with (as though God wasn't the source of it as well) and another is that God actually wanted some bad in the world (really?) and yet another is that some bad things are actually helpful (Seneca). The Stoic idea of God itself is problematic but that's for another letter.

So, my response is that, while the statement *'The universe is benevolent in its overall plan'* may be a helpful statement in therapeutic situations and even in many general situations, it cannot be considered a rational statement. If it is not rational, then I have a problem basing a system of thought on it.

The universe is benevolent: Gem or a cobweb?

The universe is benevolent in its overall plan. Gem or a cobweb?

For a helping professional, perhaps a gem. For a rational inquirer, it is an unproven assumption and hence not a gem.

Hope this makes sense.

LETTER 6. TIM TO CHUCK

 I like your approach. I am happy to take up your idea and go through the SABS Stoic worldview statements one by one and think together about whether each is a gem or cobweb. Then we can come back to the ethics and psychology.

Is the universe benevolent?

So, here is my view on,

The universe is benevolent in its overall plan.

I don't see any evidence that the universe has a plan or even is the kind of thing that can have a plan. I don't see how the universe can be seen as being entirely benevolent. So, definitely these statements have to count as 'not proven'. But should we go further? A lot of statements that are probably false like 'there is a pot of gold at the end of my garden' are also unproven – so, yes, I would go further and say 'not proven and no reason to think it is true'.

As to whether it is therapeutic, well, I suppose it could be. Martin Seligman and other positive psychologists have evidence for the benefits of optimism.[36] The Stoic view about the universe is the kind of idea that helped keep Viktor Frankl going in the concentration camps – though it must have been sorely tested! It surely helped Marcus Aurelius in his melancholier moments.

This view might help someone who has suffered a great loss become reconciled to their fate. A good example comes from Frankl who treated a widower overcome with grief that his wife had died. Frankl asked the man "how would she have coped if you had died first?" and, according to Frankl, it was a one-question cure. The widower replied "Of course, she would have suffered terribly" and left the office much happier.

But I am not certain it is a good idea to base therapy on ideas that are probably false. What do we say when the client comes back next week and says, "But why did she have to die so soon – and so painfully?".

Personally, I would prefer to argue as follows: Unfortunately, the universe has no plan – unless we stretch the meaning of 'plan' to include the Darwinian 'plan' for genes to survive. Although overall life is a great good, there are plenty of terrible things happening. Bad things happen to good people.

We cannot always stop adverse events happening, but we can control how we respond to them. Let's return to Frankl's patient, the grieving widower. What would be a good way for him to respond to his loss? We could suggest some of the following:

- Mourn his loss.
- Honour his wife's memory to keep it alive.
- Avoid ruminating on how unfair it was that his wife should die.
- Adapt to his new life situation (after the passage of time to mourn).

So, in the case of loss, I think we can argue that the above ideas – based on the dichotomy of control and Stoic ethics – are sufficient without relying on the idea that the universe is benevolent.

The universe is benevolent: Gem or a cobweb?

To sum up: As far as acceptability or truth-value, this statement is at best unproven and probably false. As to whether it is helpful or of therapeutic value, I would argue that though it could be useful on certain occasions, it is risky to base what we do on false premises. Stoic ethics can lead to wise action.

So, it turns out on this one I am perhaps more 'radical' than you, Chuck. I think it's a cobweb, and in my book, the score is Stoic Ethics, 1; Stoic Physics, 0.

I don't know if you would disagree or have any further thoughts on the above?

Is the Universe a Living Thing?

LETTER 7. CHUCK TO TIM

The 'truthiness' of received wisdom

I am glad you are more radical than me although I don't consider myself that radical. I just don't like repeating statements because they *sound wise* and impressive. It is surprising – or perhaps not – how many people are quick to attribute my contrarian views to my ignorance (especially in social media) rather than to my possibly taking the time to think through them. We easily buy into slogans and ideas that sound true without giving too much thought to them – we tend to depend on the 'truthiness' (as comedian Stephen Colbert would call it) rather than on the truth.

One that readily comes to mind is Socrates' famous, but rather absurd, dictum admiringly quoted by many: "An unexamined life is not worth living." Really? Why not? What arrogance is it to assume that we can decide whose life is worth living and whose is not? Why isn't the life of a non-introspective person worth living? Aren't we all descendants of people whose main concern was just to survive rather than to 'examine their lives'? Wouldn't it be more appropriate to say that 'an unexamined statement is not worth repeating'?

When we examine a statement like 'the universe is benevolent', we see it as a non-rational one. However, it may be beneficial for people to believe that the universe is benevolent rather than malevolent, since psychologists tell us that optimism is more beneficial than pessimism. Yet, in the final analysis, I can't take issue with you when you point out that it may not be a good idea to use a non-rational idea even in a therapeutic context.

Is the universe a living thing?

Now to another of the statements you want me to address,

The universe is a living thing.

Is the idea true?

The universe is "the totality of all space and time; all that is, has been, and will be."[37] Is this a living thing? Many pantheists thought so. Many adherents of the modern Gaia hypothesis[38] [39] think so as well. But I don't believe that there is any evidence that this is so. Since the universe is the totality of everything alive and everything that isn't, what does it even mean to say that it is alive? Is everything that is not alive in the universe alive because the universe itself is alive? Or do dead things remain dead like dead cells do in a living body? It leads to unanswerable questions like:

> *If it is alive, is it conscious?*
>
> *If it conscious, is it benevolent or malevolent?*
>
> *If it is one or the other, is it intelligent or stupid?'*
>
> *If it is living, should we expect it to die like all other living organisms?*

As far as I know, science doesn't support the idea that the universe is a living thing.

Is the idea beneficial?

Is the idea beneficial? It could be, if it is understood metaphorically rather than literally. Recalling from memory, somewhere in his book *Perennial Philosophy*,[40] Aldous Huxley makes the point that viewing things as sacred leads to a happier life. When we view the universe as a living thing and therefore sacred and do not hurt it by polluting it and misusing its resources, it could be beneficial to us all. (I am, of course, assuming that we generally believe life to be more sacred than non-life and so generally treat it better.)

The universe is a living thing. Gem or cobweb?

The universe is a living thing. Gem or cobweb?

From a rational perspective, a cobweb. From a beneficial perspective, maybe not a cobweb, *if* interpreted metaphorically rather than literally.

LETTER 8. TIM TO CHUCK

Is the Universe a Living thing?

Thanks for your latest – this is proving a very interesting discussion. Today I am sending you my thoughts on,

The universe is a living thing. Gem or cobweb?

I find this harder to answer. A year ago, I would have had no hesitation in depositing this item in the box marked cobwebs. Since then, I have spent a very interesting few months discussing Spinoza's *Ethics* with a friend[41] and have become more open to the idea that what common sense tells us and what is actually the case may be two quite different things. So, with an open mind, I want to ask – is it true?

A lot of serious thinkers are wondering if the universe may be in some sense a living thing.

Panpsychism

For example, look at the renewed interest in Panpsychism, that "the doctrine or belief that everything material, however small, has an element of individual consciousness".[42] The view has a long and venerable history in philosophical traditions of both East and West and has recently enjoyed a revival in analytic philosophy. For its proponents, panpsychism offers an attractive middle way between physicalism on the one hand and dualism on the other. The worry with dualism—the view that mind and matter are fundamentally different kinds of thing—is that it leaves us with a radically disunified picture of nature, and the deep difficulty of understanding how mind and brain interact. And whilst physicalism offers a simple and unified vision of the world, this is arguably at the cost of being unable to give a satisfactory account of the emergence of human and animal consciousness. Panpsychism, strange as it sounds on first hearing, promises a satisfying account of the human mind within a unified conception of nature.[43]

Philosophers Thomas Nagel and David Chalmers are sympathetic to this view, Chalmers because he does not see other options solving the 'hard' question of consciousness.

Gaia hypothesis

James Lovelock and others have put forward the controversial Gaia hypothesis[44], which proposes that living organisms interact with their inorganic surroundings on Earth to form a synergistic and self-regulating complex system that helps to maintain and perpetuate the conditions for life on the planet.[45]

Biocentrism

Then we have serious scientists who argue, as the ancient Stoics did, that the universe is a living thing. For example, Robert Lanza, author of *Biocentrism*, has written,

> *Our individual separateness in space and time ... is, in a sense, illusory. We are all melted together, parts of an organism that transcends the walls of space and time. This is not, you understand, a fanciful metaphor. It is a reality. I have learned, as a biologist and biocentrist, that life is a complex play of cells, some that are around when you're young, some when you're old, but that all, regardless of species, are parts of one organism expanding and contracting in space and time in whatever shape and form it can.*[46]

Philosophers and scientists

So, we have serious contemporary thinkers in both philosophy and science arguing for the Stoic idea that the universe is a living thing. Of course, serious thinkers argue for all sorts of positions, this does not make it true! Unfortunately, I don't have the expertise to investigate or unravel the above arguments. So, I will choose an agnostic position. Maybe the universe is a living thing, maybe not.

Is it helpful to think of the universe as a living thing? Quite possibly. It will help us feel connected with others. It may even help us save the planet. Even if we keep the idea at a metaphorical level, it will be helpful.

The universe is a living thing. Gem or cobweb?

The universe is a living thing. Gem or cobweb?

Is it true? I don't know. Is it helpful? (Probably) yes.

Next up: 'The universe embodies wisdom.' – what do you think?

LETTER 9. CHUCK TO TIM

Three thousand years of 'wondering' with no resolution in sight

You say,

A lot of serious thinkers are wondering if the universe may be in some sense a living thing.

Exactly. After at least three thousand years of science and philosophy, 'serious thinkers' are still 'wondering' about something that is as basic as this. That is the nature of unanswerable questions. People come back to the same questions repeatedly with a contrary answer. If they have enough intellectual firepower they are lauded, if not, they are laughed at.

We not only do not know, but we *cannot* know.

So how do we decide whether the universe is a living thing – in fact, what is true in general? Does God exist? Do we have free will? What is consciousness? What is behind the mind-boggling harmony of the universe?

Not only do not we know, but I hold that we *cannot* know.

That does not mean that no one can convince me otherwise, but I have heard enough arguments about these questions and have thought long and hard about them to feel that we cannot know. Every single answer I have heard for questions regarding God, free will, and the nature of the universe has left me totally unconvinced. As the philosopher-poet-mathematician Omar Khayyam put it,

> Myself when young did eagerly frequent doctor and saint,
> and heard great argument about it and about;
> but evermore came out by the same door as in I went.[47]

Intellectual debates may stimulate the mind, but they don't always illuminate

You quote Lanza,

> Our individual separateness in space and time ... is, in a sense, illusory.

I have heard this from many philosophical traditions as well: J. Krishnamurti, Zen Buddhists, and many others. Still, I don't understand what it could possibly mean. When I closely follow their arguments, it seems to make sense, but when I am not thinking seriously about it, not so much. I see it and I don't. Mostly I don't. Maybe I am not sophisticated enough to understand, but I also wonder, if there is an answer, why would it be so difficult to grasp?

Sure, there are serious contemporary philosophers and scientists who argue that the universe is a living thing. So? I couldn't have put it better than you when you said,

> Of course, serious thinkers argue for all sorts of positions, this does not make it true! Unfortunately, I don't have the expertise

to investigate or unravel the above arguments. So, I will choose
an agnostic position.

I don't have the expertise to investigate or unravel the above arguments either. So, I will choose an agnostic position as well. The corollary to that is, when agnostics choose not to lean on either side, they act *as though* they favour the negative side. This is inevitable. If I don't know whether there is a God or not, I cannot act as though God exists. So, my actions will resemble those of an atheist, although I am not one. It's the same logic here. Since I don't know if the universe is a living thing because it is not proven to be so, I cannot base a system of thought on that assumption. Hence it is a cobweb, except as a metaphor.

Does the Universe Embody Wisdom?

LETTER 9 (CONTINUED). CHUCK TO TIM

The next proposition we are exploring together is,

The universe embodies wisdom.

This proposition is very intriguing to me. In general, I am in total awe of the universe I find myself in. The harmony and ferocity of nature, the breathtaking sights, the changing of seasons, the revolving of planets, an embryo developing into a grown being, the colours, the sights, the sounds, and the life forms of the universe are endless. I can watch a centipede crawl or a spider weave its web and freeze in the wonder of it all. It is hard to shake the feeling that the universe embodies incredible wisdom.

My sense of wonder about the universe is vividly captured in the following passage from William Jennings Bryan:

I have observed the power of the watermelon seed. It has the power of drawing from the ground and through itself 200,000 times its weight. When you can tell me how it takes this material and out of it colours an outside surface beyond the imitation of art, and then forms inside of it a white rind and within that again a red heart, thickly inlaid with black seeds, each one of which in turn is capable of drawing through itself 200,000 times its weight – when you can explain to me the mystery of a watermelon, you can ask me to explain the mystery of God.

Looking at all this wonder, I am tempted to say that the universe embodies an incredible amount of wisdom. But when I take a sober second look, I realize that what appears to be wisdom is my overlooking a more obvious explanation: my inability to explain many natural phenomena. How is this different from pre-scientific thinking? As an explanation of the natural phenomena, didn't people create gods in charge of things they didn't understand?

The universe may exhibit 'wisdom-like qualities' but it does not embody wisdom

Indeed, the universe exhibits wisdom-like qualities. It also exhibits vice-like qualities. When we say that 'the universe embodies wisdom', we are attributing human qualities to the universe with no evidence it can know what is wise and what is vicious and chooses to be wise.

The universe embodies wisdom.
A cobweb or a gem?

As a basis for building a reliable system of thought, not a gem. But I believe that a sense of wonder is a great thing to have. When that sense of wonder is so overpowering and inspires awe in us, maybe we can be forgiven for temporarily believing that the universe embodies wisdom, as long as we don't go about basing our life on that.

LETTER 10. TIM TO CHUCK

 Thank you for your latest. It was most thought-provoking. So much so, that in this letter I am not even going to get to talking about whether the universe embodies wisdom. I will get on to that next time, I hope. Here I want to go back to the proposition that the universe is a living thing.

I am not so sure. Let's think about it in the context of less contentious issues – my daily train commute. Will my train be delayed? I don't know. I am neither a believer who commits to the idea that 'it will be delayed' nor a sceptic (akin to the atheist who doesn't believe in train delays) who commits to 'my train won't be delayed'. I am agnostic. Do I then act like a sceptic? Not at all. I realize that my train being delayed is a possibility. In this case I act more like a believer – I leave plenty of contingency time.

We could say that in situations like this where we do not know, we need to act as *rational agents facing uncertainty*. In this case, I (and others) lose much less by leaving 20 minutes early than I would by missing client meetings. It is rational for me to act like someone who believes in train delays, though actually I am agnostic.

We might translate this to talk about probabilities and utilities. The result would be the same. There is a significant probability (though less than 50%) of train delays, a substantial loss if I don't act on this possibility, so it's rational for me to leave early.

So, my thinking the train could be delayed is *not a cobweb* in my system of thinking and behaviour, far from it. In a like manner, I wonder if 'the universe being a living thing' should not be considered a cobweb. We don't know if it's true, but *it could be*. It's hard to quantify the probability, but it's not zero. It may even be quite high.

Let's do a cost-benefit analysis of this belief. If it turns out to be true, then ignoring it will mean I am likely to do the universe harm. If the universe is a living thing, then its welfare and flourishing is surely very important, so to take care of it is very important. I am sure this has considerable significance with regards to how we treat the planet and ecosystem. So, when I consider whether to take the car rather than the train, I should bear in mind that I am possibly harming a living thing by polluting the atmosphere. If it turns out not to be a living thing, then, rather like me leaving contingency time for my train journey, the subsequent loss is justified given the risk of a train delay (or the universe being a living thing).

I got thinking, "Hold on, is it even true that if I was a sceptic about the universe being a living thing, then it's necessarily a cobweb? Aren't there things we know to be false, but which we are well-advised to believe?"

For example, to continue the theme of my daily commute, I regularly set my watch to be three minutes fast. So, when I look at my watch, it's wrong. I believe it to be three minutes later than it is. Why do I do this? Because it means I am more likely to catch my train. So, although I am deliberately believing something false (that it is three minutes later than it is), this is helpful, it's not a cobweb.

In the same way, even if I don't believe the universe is a living thing, it may be helpful for me to think of it in this way. It may also be helpful for me to encourage others to think this way. Plato[48] would remind us of the value of a "noble lie".

If the above is right, then 'the universe is a living thing' is not a cobweb. It also means we should not be too hasty in moving from 'I don't think it's true' to 'it's a cobweb'.

What do you think?

LETTER 11. CHUCK TO TIM

That was a fascinating letter. It helped me clarify my thinking. You raise many interesting issues. Let me see if I am up to answering them satisfactorily.

What if it turns out that the universe is a living thing?

You then point out the benefits of believing that the universe is a living thing:

> If [that the universe is a living thing] turns out to be true, then ignoring it will mean I am likely to do the universe harm. If the universe is a living thing, then its welfare and flourishing is surely very important, so to take care of it is very important. I am sure this has considerable significance with regards to how we treat the planet and ecosystem.

I don't think that you need to believe that the universe is a living thing to not harm it. I don't believe my house is a living thing either. But that doesn't persuade me to vandalize it.

Finally, you make a case for the belief that the universe is a living thing based on its benefits:

> Don't we deliberately choose to believe what we know to be false? Aren't there things we know to be false, but which we are well-advised to believe? For example, to continue the theme of my daily commute, I regularly set my watch to be three minutes fast. So, when I look at my watch, it's wrong. I believe it to be three minutes later than it is. Why do I do this? Because it means I am more likely to catch my train. So, although I am deliberately believing something false (that it is three minutes later than it is), this is helpful, it's not a cobweb.

I agree with the idea that some irrational beliefs can be useful. If you will recall, I made exactly the same point in my earlier letter (fifth in the series),

> There are beneficial statements that may not be true and true statements that may not be beneficial.

Similarly, the belief that the universe is a living thing can be considered 'helpful' by some. If someone believes that the idea 'the universe is a living thing' is helpful to them, why should I object to it? Some non-rational beliefs can be helpful. However, would I build a philosophy of life on non-rational beliefs because they are 'helpful'? I don't think so. Here's why.

Belief in a statement like 'the universe is a living thing' in itself may be harmless and even beneficial. What we derive from it when we accept it as truth may not be. For example, if the universe is a living thing, should it be accorded all the protections that we give to living beings? Should pollution be treated as willful harming of a living being, punishable with incarceration? Should those who 'harm' the universe be liable for criminal prosecution? Should those who use the resources of the universe without paying back anything be considered thieves?

There is a big difference between accepting something untrue because it is expedient to do so and treating it as literally true. The former is a tentative assumption with predictable consequences while the latter can lead potentially to a warped way of looking at things with unpredictable consequences. We cannot equate tentative assumptions with fundamental beliefs.

Yes, people should be free to believe in God, demons, angels, the tooth fairy, ET, living earth, or flat earth. If it helps them, who are we to object? And yet, the fact that it accords comfort to some does not make it true. What cannot be shown to be true cannot create a solid foundation for the house of Stoicism or for any other rational philosophy of life.

LETTER 12. TIM TO CHUCK

 First, some thoughts on your most interesting reply. I think our main areas of difference here may be on the agnostic/atheist perspective regarding theoretical rather than empirical uncertainties. I still believe that we should base theoretical uncertainties on a balance of probabilities, given our understanding, whether or not we are in a position to discover if they are true. So, I am going to stick to my line that I would need to spend a lot more time trying to understand the theories I mentioned a couple of letters back.

Does this mean we should act as if the universe is a living thing? I am not sure, but, again, given the lack of power of other strategies to help people be more environmentally aware – perhaps we do! A speaker at the London Stoicon-X in 2019 made similar points about how we need to adopt an attitude of love to the universe. But perhaps we can agree that seeing this statement as *metaphorically* true is sufficient.

I am really not sure what to make of the prospective cobweb or gem that you began to discuss your earlier letter – that the universe embodies wisdom. I struggle to understand what it even means.

- What does *wisdom* mean? My dictionary says that it is "the quality of having experience, knowledge, and good judgment".

- What does *embody* mean? Here my dictionary says, "to express, personify, or exemplify in concrete form".

Putting these two definitions together, we get the following: *The universe expresses, personifies, or exemplifies in concrete form the quality of having experience, knowledge, and good judgment.*

I am still not sure what to make of this statement!

Can you help me understand what this statement really means? What do the ancient Stoics thinks counts in its favour? What would count as an example of the universe embodying wisdom? As you can probably tell, I'm inclined towards the cobweb view, but I'd like to be able to look at the other side of the argument – if I knew what it was! Help!

Does the Universe Embody Wisdom? [2]

LETTER 13. CHUCK TO TIM

Do we care more for possessions?

Maybe my views are coloured by my observation that, in general, people are not rational. I tend to believe that people are more caring of non-living things (such as their possessions) than they are of other living beings. I see so much unnecessary cruelty against animals and our fellow human beings that I find it hard to believe that people would treat the earth any better if they thought it was a living being. But I am also aware that my views, in most cases, tend to be those of the minority.

Does the universe embody wisdom?

Let's move on to the question,

Does the universe embody wisdom?

I have some sympathy with this idea in the sense that the universe resembles the acts of a being with enormous wisdom. The incredible harmony of the universe – the sun providing us light, the way our bodies restore themselves while we sleep, how an embryo becomes a full-fledged animal or a human being, how we are endowed with senses, the beauty of nature, the grace of animals ... I can go on and on. I am an early riser and most days I get up by 4 or 5 am. As I look out of my window, I see the majesty, grandeur, and the beauty of the rising sun. The colours and glow are breathtaking. No great artist can replicate this. The universe fills me with wonder and a major part of that wonder is the harmony – and hence the wisdom-like appearance – of the universe.

If, as you say, to 'embody' means 'to express, personify, or exemplify in concrete form', the universe does express, personify, or exemplify wisdom-like qualities in concrete form.

I said, 'wisdom-like' qualities. But is it wisdom?

Again, I look at your definition of wisdom as 'the quality of having experience, knowledge, and good judgment'. 'Good judgment' implies a conscious evaluation of alternatives. Is the universe conscious and capable of evaluating alternatives? I don't believe so. In the absence of convincing evidence to the contrary, I fall back on my agnostic way of looking at things: I don't know. When I don't know, I cannot possibly attribute wisdom to the universe.

So, to the question, 'Does the universe embody wisdom?' my answer is no, even though I believe the universe does exhibit wisdom-like qualities. So, it is not a gem. Personally though, I can't think of it as a cobweb either. And that may be because of the continual state of wonder that the universe instills in me by the way it functions. I know that not everyone shares this sense of wonder and many may find it even ridiculous.

LETTER 14. TIM TO CHUCK

Maybe I am over-optimistic in thinking that viewing the universe as a living thing is going to motivate people to treat it better. Maybe this is a more helpful metaphor,

The universe is a house which allows us to enjoy ourselves and so we shouldn't trash it.

Or maybe, in tune with Stoic thinking, we could encourage people to cultivate a philosophy of love.

Does the universe embody wisdom?

I wonder if instead, the universe embodies a struggle for survival and the passing on of those genes most fit for survival. This Darwinian view would see wisdom in those who *rise above* this natural struggle. Socrates, for example, thought we had to think for ourselves, and to think in an uncommonly rigorous manner to arrive at wisdom.

What if the universe may essentially have arisen for no purpose, with everything in it struggling to survive – and at the same time we have the ability, through our capacity for reason, to transcend this?

- We have the capacity to see *other people* as being essentially like us.
- We have the capacity see *animals* as sharing our capacity to suffer.
- We have the capacity to see the *whole universe* as a system that needs our attention for it to survive.

According to this view, if we try to read wisdom off from the way the universe operates, we will not get very far. When we view the universe, as well as sunshine, happiness, and altruism, we also see plague, random tragedies, and human and animal misery. Wisdom lies in making sense of this and in trying to understand what matters and how to attain it.

In this line of thinking I have been influenced by Robert Wright's excellent book, *Why Buddhism is True*.[49] Wright, an evolutionary psychologist, argues that evolution is actually the 'bad guy' in the sense that it has 'created' human beings who are in many ways misguided and certainly not programmed for happiness. Just one example is our tendency towards anxiety and our negativity bias. Those of our ancestors who were *more* attuned to danger would be much more likely to pass on their genes than those who were chilled, laid back, and positive. So, we, their survivors, have genes that make us prone to anxiety and have a negativity bias.

Yet in the twenty-first century we are actually much less subject to immediate threats of death from predators than in ancestral times, when our gene pool was formed. So, nature has given us a particularly *unhelpful* steer in this regard. We will be more anxious than we need to be for survival, let alone for happiness. Wright argues that this isn't just true about anxiety, it is also true regarding our sense of self and the nature of reality. Wisdom does not lie in reading off wisdom from the universe as it appears to us, it lies in going beyond this.

Living organisms will *not* then naturally embody wisdom, instead they (naturally) embody ideas skewed to help them pass on their genes. Wisdom lies in seeing beyond survival and genes, in thinking about what matters most in life and how to achieve it. So, while we might see admirable traits in bees or ants who co-operate, we could just as easily see hundreds more examples of animals whose behaviour we would not be wise to emulate – the praying mantis, who eats her mate, being one such example!

On balance, I don't think that it is helpful to say that the universe embodies wisdom. The universe is awe-inspiring and sometimes we can see wisdom in how it operates, but this not reliably the case.

What were the ancient Stoics thinking then, when they said that the universe embodies wisdom? Perhaps it is the logical conclusion of the Stoic physics and cosmology? If the universe is a living thing and has a providential plan, then it would certainly *need* to embody wisdom. *If* the universe embodies wisdom, it would certainly help Stoics accept their fate when things go wrong. It fits well with the Stoic philosophy of *amor fati*. 'Everyone is for the best in the best of all possible worlds'.

But from a Darwinian perspective, the universe is not like this. There is both randomness and a tendency for genes to shape us into beings fit for survival – actually, fit for survival in pre-historic times. My view is that we need to use our ability to reason to make sense of life and potentially rise above the rather selfish and materialistic inclination given to us by nature.

I am not sure I have done justice to the view that 'the universe embodies wisdom' and perhaps have argued against a slightly different proposition, that living beings embody wisdom, or that human nature embodies wisdom. Perhaps the above is more an argument against one interpretation of the Stoic view that we should live 'according to nature'. But, as I said in my previous letter, I struggle to make sense of the meaning of the phrase 'the universe embodies wisdom'.

This leads to the next question: *What did the ancient Stoics really think about God?* So, what do *you* think they thought? I would like to start with a statement you made in your earlier letters:

> *I will choose an agnostic position as well. The corollary to that is, when agnostics choose not to lean on either side, they act as though they favour the negative side. This is inevitable. If I don't know whether there is a God or not, I cannot act as though God exists. So, my actions will resemble those of an atheist, although I am not one. It's the same logic here. Since I don't know if the universe is a living thing because it is not*

proven to be so, I cannot base a system of thought on that assumption. Hence it is a cobweb, except as a metaphor.

My next question to you: Does the agnostic position mean acting like an atheist?

Does an agnostic behave like an atheist?

LETTER 15. CHUCK TO TIM

Does an agnostic behave like an atheist?

 You asked,

Does the agnostic position mean acting like an atheist?

I am not quite saying that. What I am saying is that that would be the default position. Let me use your daily commute example. When I go out on my commute, it is quite possible that there is a terrorist waiting to blow up the train, with me in it. But I don't go out thinking this could happen (although it could) and take all precautions that I would take if I thought it was *likely* to happen. It is my estimate of probability and not the possibility that would drive my decision. The idea that God exists as a possibility does not persuade me to arrange my life to conform to that possibility. So, an agnostic tends to act like an atheist although she is not one.

Doesn't an agnostic act like a believer?

You then make your point with this example,

> *Let's think about it in the context of less contentious issues – my daily train commute! Will my train be delayed? I don't know. I am neither a believer who commits to the idea that 'it will be delayed' nor a sceptic (akin to the atheist who doesn't believe in train delays) who commits to 'my train won't be delayed'. I am agnostic. Do I then act like a sceptic? Not at all. I realize that my train being delayed is a possibility. In this case I act more like a believer – I leave plenty of contingency time.*

Yes, absolutely, and I would do the same. But I believe that there are a couple of differences between this and things like believing in God. We have actually *seen* or *known* instances where trains were late or early, *as a matter of fact*, not as a matter of theoretical possibility. I adjust my behaviour accordingly – go early to the station if missing the train has undesirable consequences. It is based on my *imperfect knowledge of the future* and *its possible consequences,* and not on a theoretical possibility.

Did the Ancient Stoics Believe in God?

LETTER 16. CHUCK TO TIM

What did ancient Stoics think of God?

 You asked me,

What did ancient Stoics really think of God?

A lot of modern Stoics gloss over this question by conveniently calling the ancient Stoics 'pantheists' and therefore when they referred to God they were just referring to Nature.

I beg to differ. Big time. In fact, this question raises two issues.

1. Did the ancient Stoics believe in God (as we understand the term now)?

2. If they did, is their belief incidental to or an integral part of Stoic ethics?

I believe these issues are important because most of us in the modern Stoic movement are not professional philosophers but people who want to apply Stoic ethics to our daily lives. If the ancient Stoics were theists and if their theism was an essential part of Stoicism, then it would imply that you must believe in God to practice Stoic ethics. This would exclude atheists and agnostics from practicing Stoic ethics.

It also has a bearing on the Stoic Attitudes and Behaviours Scale (SABS) issues we have been discussing in the past several letters. Much of SABS statements can be traced back to a Stoic worldview rooted in Stoic physics.

Let's examine these two propositions. (In this letter, I will examine the first one, 'Did the ancient Stoics believe in God?')

Were the ancient Stoics theists?

The answer I hear most frequently from modern Stoics is that the ancient Stoics were not theists but *pantheists* in that they did not distinguish between God and Nature. So, the argument put forth by many modern Stoics is that, when Stoics used the term 'God', they did not really mean God but just Nature. This point of view is summarized succinctly by John Sellars,

> If 'God' is simply another name for Nature then it doesn't really do much work in their philosophy; it doesn't add or explain anything, so one might easily drop the word without any obvious loss.[50]

If this were in fact the case, then we can truly consider Stoic physics as agnostic or non-theistic. Many modern Stoics seem to assume that pantheism and theism are mutually exclusive and therefore ancient Stoics were not theists.

Pantheism does not exclude theism

But is this true? Are pantheism and theism mutually exclusive? I don't think so. As a matter of fact, A.A. Long (2002) believes that,

> As originally propounded, Stoic theology was a complex amalgam of pantheism and theism.[51]

Pantheism describes only the *form* in which God is perceived. Many theist philosophies (such as the Advaita philosophy of Hinduism, Sufism of Islam, and some forms of Kabbalah of Judaism) see God as a separate entity who is also an immanent being. Given all this, I think both theism and agnosticism are both compatible with pantheism.

- The *agnostic* pantheist equates Nature with God. (God is immanent in nature and is not outside of it.)
- The *theist* pantheist sees God both as Nature itself and also as a being outside of Nature. (God is both immanent *and* transcendent.)[52]

Therefore, to say that Stoics were pantheists does not resolve the issue at all. We need to understand *what type of pantheist* they were. Were they theists or nontheists?

My view is that many of them were theists. My reasoning is as follows.

Ancient Stoics attributed qualities of 'God' to 'Nature'

Zeno developed several syllogisms[53] to support the idea that the universe is rational, wise, eternal, and perceiving which also forms the basis for several SABS statements.

As the Stoic scholar David Sedley of Cambridge points out,

> The Stoic God is a single cause of everything ... He is, further, a supremely intelligent, good and provident being who plans and necessitates the world's entire development from beginning to end.[54]

If the universe is "wise, eternal, and perceiving", and if the Stoic God "plans everything from beginning to end," then I have to disagree with the interpretation that God is just another word for Nature, as the quote from John Sellars would suggest. Nature as we know it does not have these attributes. No modern scientist would attribute these qualities to nature. It seems then, that in Stoic theory, *God then is not another name for what we call nature as many modern Stoics suggest, but the Stoic term Nature is another name for what we call God.*

This view is further confirmed by Epictetus.

> How else could things happen with such precise regularity, if God weren't issuing orders? He orders plants to bloom and they bloom. He tells them to bear fruit and they do so... How else to explain the waxing and waning of the moon, coming and going of the sun, and changes and fluctuations on earth?[55]

God "issues orders", "tells plants to bloom and they bloom", and "tells them to bear fruit and they do so". It seems Epictetus was also describing a Judeo-Christian god-like entity and not nature as we understand it.

Similar views were also expressed by Marcus Aurelius, although in a decidedly less clear-cut way. Consider this passage from *Meditations*,

If one of the gods informed you, 'You will die tomorrow or, at any rate, the day after tomorrow', you would consider it no great matter...[56]

This statement implies that God is an entity who can potentially tell you something. To have this capability, God must be conceived as a transcendental entity rather than an immanent being. We can find many such ambiguous descriptions of God in *Meditations*.

And this from the Stoic philosopher Hierocles,

Though the gods are not the causes of evil, yet they connect certain persons with things of this kind and surround those who deserve [to be afflicted] with corporeal and external detriments.[57]

Gods don't cause evil, but "surround those who deserve it" with "corporeal and external detriments". Again, not unlike a Judeo-Christian God.

Cleanthes was also clearly a theistic pantheist. His hymn to Zeus implicitly assumes a transcendental God.

As far as I can tell, Tim, many ancient Stoics would be considered theists in modern parlance because they attributed qualities of what we would call God to what they called Nature. A.A. Long's view, which I quoted earlier, is in line with this. Therefore, I believe that Stoic pantheism, in many cases, is just theism in a different form. Only the form of God changes, God remains. We will see the implication of this to Stoic ethics later. Meanwhile, I would like to know your thoughts on this.

LETTER 17. TIM TO CHUCK

 Many thanks for your latest thought-provoking installment.

It's an area again which I would imagine would be open to different interpretations, and as neither of us claim to be experts on the original texts, perhaps a degree of tentativeness would be wise here. I have to say, though, that I have always thought of the ancient Stoics as *theistic pantheists*, so I agree with you on that. *If* this is right, then the Stoic system becomes more self-supporting than otherwise.

I think it goes like this:

1. The logos (Reason) rules the universe.
2. The universe has a benign purpose. (Here the Stoics disagree with Spinoza.)
3. We should follow Reason (and whatever the universe decides is our fate).

In the memorable analogy of the dog and cart, we should follow the cart (Reason) rather than struggle against it. All is for the best anyway since God/Zeus is wise and benevolent. So, when something apparently bad befell Marcus Aurelius, he was able to say that it was part of the great web, all part of God's plans – it isn't really bad, in the grand scale of things, regardless of how things might seem to us with our limited perspective.

Things get a bit confusing for me when some Stoics start to talk about Zeus. It's easy here to think of Zeus as being very similar to the Judeo-Christian God. Indeed, this is what Mark Vernon argued in his debate with me on the subject in the *Modern Stoicism* forum some time ago.[58] You (and our readers) might like to read Mark Vernon's thoughts. Chuck, you might even want to discuss the debate between myself and Vernon in your next reply. I wonder if you will agree with me that the theistic version of pantheism is a cobweb.

Perhaps some of the early Christians were influenced by the Stoic view of God and transported some elements of Stoicism into Christianity? Certainly, Cleanthes' *Hymn to Zeus*[59] – which, incidentally, adds extra support to your view that the ancient Stoics were theists – resembles the Lord's Prayer in structure, and we know the direction of any possible causation!

I've just read A.A Long on the topic.[60] Long says that there is a tension between the theist and pantheist elements in Stoicism. He says that most Stoics had elements of both, and that Epictetus and Cleanthes tended more towards the theist view. The pantheists see God as immanent; the theists see God as transcendent. For the pantheists, there are a few puzzles – why do the Stoics say that only we (humans) partake of reason, if God is everywhere?

Both the theists and pantheists would say that God makes a difference. As I argued above, even on the pantheist view, if the logos rules the universe, and we see God as a kind of universal mind immanent in everything, then it helps us accept everything and remain optimistic.

Perhaps the main difference is in our attitude to prayer. Cleanthes and Epictetus imply that prayer to God is worthwhile. Zeus can intervene. On the pantheistic view, prayer is pointless as God is just the laws of nature or the law of reason.

Have you got specific examples of what other Modern Stoics have written that would contradict my interpretation? I believe that many prominent modern Stoics such as Donald Robertson would not argue too much with the above. They would, I think, say that we are better off without either pantheism or theism. If my understanding is correct, they would think they are cobwebs and that you can construct a viable Modern Stoicism without either. That's what I think too.

LETTER 18. CHUCK TO TIM

This is brilliant. I hadn't read your debate with Mark Vernon before this, but that's exactly what I have been trying to get at from the beginning.

God or human judgment?

Vernon's argument is that, because ancient Stoics were theists, everything – including the Stoic dichotomy – is subject to God's will. Therefore, it is God – not our reasoning faculty – that is at the core of Stoicism and "We are interpreters of God's world and witnesses of God's work".[61] You counter this by saying that modern Stoicism overcomes this problem by severing the connection between Stoic theism and Stoic ethics, by pruning what is not acceptable and what is not useful.

A third (outlandish?) perspective

Let me propose a third alternative.

> *There never, ever was a true and undisputed connection between Stoic physics (which is the basis of Stoic God) and Stoic ethics.*

If Plotinus[62] had not already said it, I could have said,

> *[The Stoics] bring in God for the sake of appearances.*

If John Sellars had not already said it, I could have said,

[God] doesn't really do much work in [Stoic] philosophy; it doesn't add or explain anything, so one might easily drop the word without any obvious loss. [63]

If Brad Inwood had not already said it, I could have said,

The narrow focus on ethical improvement is also an authentic component of ancient Stoicism. [64]

If Julia Annas had not already said it, I could have said,

We find no texts in which virtue, impulse, and the like are derived from Stoic physics. [65]

Why am I making the claim that Stoic physics and metaphysics have no real connection to Stoic ethics? Why am I saying that, for all practical purposes, Stoic ethics is Stoicism? Why am I saying that you don't have to sever the connection between Stoic physics and ethics, because there was never one to begin with?

But first, let me answer the question whether this claim is as outrageous as it sounds. Let us look at this more closely. Stoic theism arises out of Stoic physics, the Stoic view of how things work. Stoic physics, which included metaphysics and theology, is more than what we would call physics. Many ancient Stoics seemed to have considered Stoic physics as an integral part of Stoicism without which there was no foundation for Stoic ethics. It is Stoic physics (along with Stoic logic) that is supposed to nurture Stoic ethics.

A fundamental aspect of Stoic philosophy is the twofold idea that ethics is central to the effort, and that the study of ethics is to be supported by two other fields of inquiry, what the Stoics called 'logic' and 'physics'. [66]

Once we agree that Stoic physics is the basis of Stoic ethics, then Vernon's argument can be assumed to follow logically from that. Stoicism becomes another religion rather than a rational way of looking at things. This is the problem I have with Stoic physics. I simply don't believe that Stoicism is just another religion and not a self-contained rational philosophy of life.

But I acknowledge that my beliefs don't make things true or false. My beliefs, to have any validity at all, have to be supported by logic, empirical evidence, or both.

I don't want to make this letter too long, though. So, I will outline the reasons that led me up to the conclusion that Stoic physics, metaphysics, and gods have never been relevant to Stoic ethics in my next letter.

LETTER 19. FROM TIM TO CHUCK

One of my favourite ways of spending an evening is to have a philosophical dinner with a friend, sometimes a group of friends. We eat well, drink a glass or two of wine to help the flow of conversation, and discuss or debate philosophy (sometimes after choosing a topic in advance). I like to imagine our discussion in such a setting. If it were, we would now be reaching the cigar and port stage.

I imagine hearing your latest thoughts, taking a puff of the cigar (metaphorically, but it would be one of those occasions when I wish I did smoke!), and a sip of port. Probably an eyebrow would be raised. Maybe I would start to put together some thoughts, perhaps arguing for my position, which you correctly sum up in your last letter.

What I hope I would do, however, would be to ask you to elaborate. You have my attention. So, whilst I take another sip of port (OK, in real life it's coffee), take your time, the ball is in your court.

Is Stoic Physics the Foundation or a Pedestal?

LETTER 20. CHUCK TO TIM[67]

I like your setting of an evening with a glass of port and a cigar. It's in line with my thinking.

On the emperor and his clothes

I generally confine my arguments to simple logic and observations. I do not profess to have an in-depth knowledge of philosophy and an uncanny ability to endlessly split hairs (although my ability to split infinitives is unquestioned). I try to avoid terms like 'pre-Cartesian', 'post-Hegelian', 'Einsteinian', and other such non-specific references to observations not in evidence. Neither of us is a professional philosopher, and even if we were, I hope we don't hide under the cloak of scholarship and obfuscate. (I admire people like Brad Inwood, A.A. Long, Chris Gill, and David Sedley for their clarity of exposition, even while discussing complex topics.) I believe that basic concepts of any subject can be logically explained to, understood, and challenged by any serious inquirer.

I have always been a fan of 'the father of nuclear physics' Ernest Rutherford's observation,

> If you cannot explain what you are doing in your lab to the char [cleaner, in today's parlance], perhaps you don't know what you are doing.

Consequently, my reasons will be neither clever nor learned but very pedestrian: 'Can we just look at the emperor and see if he has any clothes?' rather than trying to resolve it through clever arguments and deductive logic.

Let's continue our fireside chat.

Stoic physics is just a pedestal

Content-wise, Stoic physics bear little resemblance to modern physics.

> Stoic physics... included theology, ontology, determinism, the nature of causation, as well as topics such as cosmology and the study of plants and animals.[68]

The idea of God as the source of everything is rooted in Stoic physics and treated as the foundation of Stoic ethics (providing the rationale for Vernon's argument that it is

God, not human judgment, that is supreme). Yet Stoic physics has never been more than a pedestal. I am not disputing John Sellar's (2015) observation,

> *The Stoics wanted to understand Nature because Nature taken as a whole is the greatest thing there is, and we are parts of it.*[69]

However, wanting to understand something and actually understanding it are two different things. The Stoics might have thought that they had identified the foundation of Stoic ethics but, in my view, what they found was just a pedestal. If Stoic physics does not form the foundation of Stoic ethics, then we don't have to be too concerned about Stoic gods either.

But, as I said earlier, my beliefs don't make what I say true or false. So, I am sure you would challenge me to explain why I believe that Stoic physics is a pedestal that can be removed without affecting Stoic ethics – and not the foundation that is essential for Stoicism.

Why Stoic physics is just a pedestal

Here are the propositions upon which I base my conclusion that Stoic physics and Stoic gods are not needed for Stoic ethics to be true. I build my arguments against Stoic physics being the foundation of Stoic ethics on seven propositions:

1. Stoic physics was challenged from the time it was introduced.
2. Even the ancient Stoics who believed in Stoic physics have unequivocally admitted that Stoic ethics would work even without Stoic physics.

3. In the past 2,000 years our understanding of physics has changed radically. Yet this had no effect on Stoic ethics.
4. There is no way one could derive Stoic ethics from Stoic physics.
5. Stoic physics cannot explain the problem of evil.
6. Studying Stoic physics sheds no light on Stoic ethics.
7. Even those who believe Stoic physics to be the basis of Stoic ethics can and do explain Stoic ethics without any reference to physics.

PROPOSITION 1.

If Stoic physics was the basis of Stoic ethics, physics would have gained universal acceptance. It didn't, almost from the day it was proposed by Zeno. Even some of Zeno's own students disputed that Stoic physics was an essential part of Stoicism.

The challenge to Stoic physics (by extension to the Stoic God) is not a modern phenomenon proposed by those who don't understand 'authentic Stoicism' (as I am often helpfully reminded by social media experts on Stoicism), and as Vernon implies. As soon as Zeno proposed Stoic physics as a necessary part of Stoicism, his student Aristo of Chios[70] who influenced Marcus Aurelius' thinking centuries later,[71] [72] rejected Stoic physics as being unnecessary. Although the far more charismatic Chrysippus (who believed in Stoic physics) won the day, the challenge remained alive during the early, middle, and late Stoas and continues to this day. Stoic physics is not a universally accepted part of Stoicism, ancient or modern.

PROPOSITION 2

Even those ancient Stoics who accepted the idea of God and other ideas of Stoic physics stated unambiguously (albeit I suspect, probably grudgingly) that Stoic ethics would work, with or without God. If they thought that Stoicism couldn't function without Stoic physics, they wouldn't have made such unequivocal comments.

This is Epictetus speaking,

What do I care whether everything that exists is made up of atoms, indivisibles, or fire and earth? ... Questions that are beyond our understanding, we should ignore.[73]

He goes on to say that it's useless to understand them even if we could.

It may well be that the human mind cannot grasp them. Even if you think they are perfectly understandable, what's the use of understanding them? Should we not say those who think these things are an essential part of a philosopher's knowledge are creating unwanted problems for themselves?[74]

Marcus Aurelius agrees. In many places in *Meditations*, he states that Stoic principles will work even if we reject its physics. For example,

Either all things proceed from one intelligent source and come together as in one body, and the part ought not to find fault with what is done for the benefit of the whole; or there are only atoms, and nothing else than mixture and dispersion. Why, then, are you disturbed?[75]

Either there is a fatal need and a law that cannot be violated, or a kind Providence, or chaos without purpose or order.[76]

While Marcus Aurelius himself believed in a universe ruled by providence, he didn't consider it a prerequisite to follow Stoic ethics.

Even Musonius Rufus talked against the unnecessary multiplicity of concepts.

PROPOSITION 3[77]

If Stoic physics were the foundation of Stoic ethics, then when the foundation shakes, so should the structure built upon it. If nothing happens to the structure (Stoic ethics) when the supposed foundation (Stoic physics) shakes or collapses, then it is unlikely to be the foundation.

In the past 2,300 years our knowledge of the universe and how it works has radically changed. In what way did this affect Stoic ethics? In what way could it even potentially affect Stoic ethics? With the notable exception of Lawrence Becker, did it even occur to any modern Stoic that we need to study modern physics for this purpose? I venture to guess probably not. If people genuinely believed that physics is the basis of Stoic ethics, I am sure they would have paid a lot more attention to modern physics.

The Stoic physics principles of theism and determinism are now – and maybe forever – unresolvable issues. Unless we claim that Stoicism is some form of religion based on having faith in unresolvable issues, Stoic physics cannot possibly be the foundation of Stoic ethics. Stoic physics principles (such as the corporeality of the soul and the origin and dissolution of the universe) are not in line with modern science.

You ask me, Tim, *"how you can justify the ethics* without *the physics?"* I wonder *how one can justify the ethics* with *the physics.*

PROPOSITION 4

If Stoic physics is the foundation of Stoic ethics, one should be able to derive (at least a part of) Stoic ethics from it and be able to demonstrate that it cannot be derived otherwise.

Some eminent Stoic scholars and philosophers have indeed *connected* Stoic physics to Stoic ethics. For example, Pierre Hadot, (who was ordained by the church), believes that the discipline of assent can be derived from Stoic physics. But his derivation is not a strict logical derivation, rather, simply an assumed connection. From a logical perspective, if A can be derived from B, it does not follow that B is indispensable for deriving A; it may simply mean a connection or an assumed relationship. Even if it can be shown that B can be logically derived from A, A is not necessarily a prerequisite for B, if B can also be shown to be logically derivable without A. *To my knowledge, Stoic scholars haven't demonstrated that Stoic ethics can ONLY be derived from Stoic physics. In fact, they have not even demonstrated that Stoic ethics can be derived from Stoic physics at all.*

Without such a demonstration, Stoic physics cannot be considered the foundation of Stoic ethics. Even if the ancient Stoics thought that Stoic ethics is an integral part of Stoic physics, as Julia Annas points out,

I don't believe that we are under any obligation to conform our use of the term 'Stoic ethics' to the ethical part of philosophy as

*understood by the Stoics themselves. I am more comfortable using **Stoic ethics as an independent area of Stoic inquiry that does not in any way depend on Stoic physics for its existence.**[78]* [Emphasis mine]

PROPOSITION 5

If we accept Stoic physics which says that Zeus was the only force, it leaves the problem of evil unexplained.

The Stoics don't have a clear answer to this. As Brad Inwood points out, their varying explanations "don't represent their finest work". [79] Their attempts to deny evil in this world by saying that the only evil in the world has to do with our judgments would mean that terrorists, child molesters, etc., are not evil but only our thinking is. Again, as Inwood says,

Such an explanation will not satisfy its critics, and neither should it.[80]

PROPOSTION 6

Understanding the theory behind something should shed light on the subject. My study of Stoic physics (which came after my study of Stoic ethics) did not offer any additional insight into Stoic ethics.

Zero. Zilch. Zippo. Nada.

I studied Stoic physics years *after* I studied Stoic ethics. My study of Stoic physics didn't make me understand Stoic ethics any better. The study of Stoic physics did not offer a single 'aha' moment with regard to Stoic ethics. As Julia Annas points out,

But if virtue, impulse, and so on are introduced in their own right from the ethical part of Stoic philosophy, we have no support for the claim that Stoic ethics can only be understood in terms of the concepts of Stoic physics.[81]

PROPOSTION 7

Even those who claim Stoic physics is foundational for the understanding of Stoic ethics are able to explain Stoic ethics 'without once bringing in pneuma or the cosmos'.

Some modern Stoics like Piotr Stankiewicz (2020) reject Stoic physics on the grounds that,

[Stoic physics isn't] *in sync with the times we live in.*[82]

without it affecting their exposition of Stoic ethics in any way. What about those that don't reject Stoic physics and embrace it as an essential part of Stoicism? It turns out that, in practice, they don't make use of Stoic physics to explain Stoic ethics either. For example, A.A. Long, one of the most respected modern Stoic scholars, maintains that Stoic physics is foundational, and "Stoic ethics should be understood in terms of Stoic physics". And yet, he goes on,

to discuss impulse, emotion, virtue, and indifferents and the other ethical topics we find in the ancient sources and do so without once bringing in pneuma or the cosmos, indeed often locating Stoic understanding of these topics in engagement with Socratic and other traditions of ethical thinking.[83]

It is tempting to believe that Stoicism derives its ethics from a comprehensive understanding of the universe. But, so far as I can see, Stoic ethics is self-contained and can be derived from self-evident principles, as A.A. Long

(1986) himself has done. It can be treated as any other branch of social science. As Julia Annas points out this is exactly what even those who believe in Stoic physics often end up doing.

How can Stoic ethics be refuted?

How then can we refute Stoic principles if we remove the foundation on which they are supposed to rest? The answer is simple. The refutation of any of the Stoic ethical principles can be done in the same way as it is done in other disciplines. There is no need to have something called 'Stoic physics' which, to my mind, is more science fiction than science. As a version of Occam's razor states, *Entia non sunt multiplicanda praeter necessitatem.*[84] There is no need to multiply the entities of thought unnecessarily. To say that Stoic physics can explain Stoic ethics is saying something more obscure can explain something less obscure.

I respectfully have to disagree with Mark Vernon's theory that God is the basis of Stoicism. I have used Stoic principles since I was a teenager without any reference to God and, as I said elsewhere,[85] they have "offered me solace when I was troubled, encouraged me when things looked bleak, and steadied me when I wobbled".

LETTER 21. TIM TO CHUCK

 The port and cigars are continuing to flow, and, although I know I should probably just sit back and ask you to finish your argument, perhaps the drink is getting to me, so I will interrupt. So here is my response to your propositions.

PROPOSITION 1.

If Stoic physics was the basis of Stoic ethics, physics would have gained universal acceptance. It didn't, almost from the day it was proposed by Zeno. Even some of Zeno's own students disputed that Stoic physics was an essential part of Stoicism.

Chuck, you offered,

There never, ever was a true and undisputed connection between Stoic physics (which is the basis of Stoic God) and Stoic ethics.

as an alternative to my view that,

Ancient Stoics believed in a worldview that is highly questionable but from which the ethics can be separated by and large intact.

So, we agree with each other and disagree with Mark Vernon on that.

Your point about Aristo is indeed an argument for the connection between physics and ethics not being *undisputed*. But that's a pretty strong demand to make – that a position has never been disputed to be part of a belief system. Sure, Aristo disputed it, I am sure others did too. But, as I pour myself another glass, I feel emboldened to argue – it remains the case that the *orthodox* Stoic views that the *majority of Stoics* held (as far as we know) were those represented by the SABS items we listed earlier (*the universe is a living thing, which embodies wisdom, and there is a rational and orderly plan in the universe and in the causes of events*). Mark Vernon argues that this view leads to the notion of a personal transcendent God outside of nature, rather like the Judeo-Christian God. Personally, I do not see this as following from the Stoic worldview. To put it in terms that Rutherford and his char would approve of:

1. Not all Stoics agreed about everything, and that's too strict a rule for something to count as being part of Stoicism.

2. Most ancient Stoics (as far as we can tell) agreed that the universe is a living thing, that it has a plan and is rational.

3. You can call this living universe 'God' or 'Zeus' if you like. It was probably very convenient for ancient Stoics to do so to avoid unnecessary prosecution or persecution. But we should avoid confusing this with a personal Judeo-Christian God.

4. The SABS items don't mention God, and I think its these *theistic* rather than non-theist, and *immanent* but not transcendent views that most Stoics were committed to, rather than the idea of a God who sits outside of nature.

So, taking another sip of port and having another puff of the cigar, I put it to you that although there wasn't a completely *undisputed* connection between physics and ethics, for most Stoics (the vast majority, as far as we know) there was indeed this connection. Which brings me back to my position when debating with Mark Vernon.[86]

PROPOSITION 3

If Stoic physics were the foundation of Stoic ethics, then when the foundation shakes, so should the structure built upon it. If nothing happens to the structure (Stoic ethics) when the supposed foundation (Stoic physics) shakes or collapses, then it is unlikely to be the foundation.

Many modern Stoics have done exactly what you say and gone with the Stoic ethics without the Stoic physics. But this doesn't resolve the question of whether the ancient Stoics saw physics as foundational. It does, however, raise the question as to how modern Stoics justify the ethics. This is the main thing I would like us to try to sort out in the rest of our exchange, before the port finally runs out.

PROPOSITION 4

If Stoic physics is the foundation of Stoic ethics, one should be able to derive (at least a part of) Stoic ethics from it and be able to demonstrate that it cannot be derived otherwise.

Spinoza thought you could construct an ethics logically, like one would mathematics. Not many commentators think he succeeded or that this is the right methodology

for ethics. Perhaps the word 'foundational' is too ambiguous. What I am thinking of, though, is something that
makes the Stoic ethics attractive, that makes it a sensible
option.[87] I think that for the ancient Stoics, the physics
and worldview made Stoic ethics make more sense.

To recap on some of my previous answer:

- If reason rules the universe, it makes sense to understand and follow reason.
- If everything is predetermined, it makes sense to
  go along with what we see as fate rather than
  struggle against it or try to change it.
- If everything is good, it makes sense to feel happy
  and optimistic even when apparently bad things
  happen.
- If we really are like brothers in that we are all part
  of the divine, it makes sense to see ourselves as
  part of a large entity rather than being separate
  entities who should just aim for their own happiness. (For example, Marcus's *Meditations* 2.1.)

But if we don't believe these things, why should we be
Stoics rather than Epicureans, Utilitarians, or Hedonists?

PROPOSITION 5

If we accept Stoic physics which says that Zeus was the only
force, it leaves the problem of evil unexplained.

As I hope I have made clear, I am not defending Stoic
physics. I am asking why we should be Stoics if we don't
believe in Stoic physics.

You write "*I respectfully have to disagree with Mark
Vernon's theory that God is the basis of Stoicism. I have*

used Stoic principles since I was a teenager without any reference to God and, as I said elsewhere, they have "offered me solace when I was troubled, encouraged me when things looked bleak, and steadied me when I wobbled."

I agree with you, Chuck, perhaps some of the ways in which Stoicism has helped you can provide an answer to my big remaining question, *why be a Stoic rather than an Epicurean (or Utilitarian, Hedonist, et cetera).*

You quote Brad Inwood: "*The narrow focus on ethical improvement is also an authentic component of ancient Stoicism.*" I think we agree on that. But it does raise what I see as the remaining big question in our exchange, as I mentioned above. 'Why *should* we focus on ethical improvement (and other aspects of Stoicism)?'

About Cicero and his motivation – I agree we can be skeptical about things that don't make sense to us. I too am skeptical about these things – we are in a lot of agreement about cobwebs. My point is that it doesn't follow that we should be skeptical about whether other people believed these things. I am skeptical about the view that the earth is the center of the universe, but this doesn't mean I should be skeptical about whether people believed this in the ancient world.

Which brings me to what for me is the key question, which has come up earlier in this letter, namely

Why should we believe in virtues as the only thing of (real) value?

I agree that virtues are good for us, in the long run. I personally would say,

If you want others to be happy, be virtuous; if you want to be happy yourself, be virtuous.

But why should anyone take my word for this? A case in point is the debate between the Epicureans and the Stoics. To the Epicureans it is self-evident that happiness and the absence of pain is desirable. Epicurus would argue that virtues are good, but only in so far as they are instrumental to happiness. He would agree with you that virtues are generally good for us and would encourage us to be virtuous. However, if we really want to feel good, why not be an Epicurean? Why not follow Epicurus rather than Epictetus and devise a non-Stoic 'discipline of desire' (as indeed Epicureans did) that means you only want to have the things that give you pleasure and no pain? Why not set up a community of like-minded people and stay away from politics? (Again, like the Epicureans.)

In short – how would you persuade Rutherford's char that Stoicism is better than Epicureanism? Why should our readers place such a high value on virtue as Stoics demand – or an even higher one as Cynics ask? Why should we place no intrinsic value on happiness?

Please forgive me, Chuck, if the port has got the better of me and that has turned into a slightly drunken rant! I'd better end with two key points:

1) Although most ancient Stoics did believe in a connection between physics and ethics, we, as modern Stoics, who do not to agree with the physics can still use the ethics.

2) But if we do so, how can we justify Stoic ethics over other ethics (such as those of Epicurus)?

Time for me to finish that glass of port and hand the conversation back to you.

LETTER 22. CHUCK TO TIM

Your counterarguments tell me that your port is excellent enough to sharpen your arguments rather than making them incoherent. I am sure the cigar is Cuban.

You introduce great arguments with which I don't necessarily disagree. And thank you for presenting your arguments in a way that conforms to the 'Rutherford & his char approved' standard.

My response to your arguments supporting Stoic physics

You make several arguments in favour of Stoic physics while commenting on my propositions. More specifically, you make the arguments that follow.

> 1. Not all Stoics agreed about everything, and that's too strict a rule for something to count as being part of Stoicism.

Agreed. One swallow does not a summer make. The point I was trying to make was that the need for Stoic physics was refuted by Zeno's own student (who was there presumably to learn from the master rather than challenge him on something as fundamental as this). Aristo became a well-known philosopher in his own right which points to his intellectual heft. Because we don't have any contemporary record of this period we don't even know if Aristo was the only dissident or whether there were many like him. We are almost exclusively relying on two non-contemporary accounts – one by Cicero, who came after all Greek Stoics were dead and gone, and another, Diogenes Laertius, who was born after all Greek *and* Roman Stoics were gone. Diogenes Laertius' account, valuable as it may be, is astonishingly anecdotal. I couldn't keep count of the number of times Diogenes Laertius prefaces what he says with, "It has been said ..." or some such phrase. Because we don't have access to any substantial original work (fragments excepted) of the Greek Stoics, practically everything we know about Greek Stoicism comes primarily from second-hand sources, especially the two mentioned above. I suspect two swallows do not make a summer either.

I have absolutely no problem conceding that not everyone needs to agree on everything. But what we are talking about is fundamental to Stoicism. The connection between Stoic physics and Stoicism was disputed from the very beginning. By how many, we don't know. All we know is by at least one. We assume that, but for this exception, there was a broad consensus. How do we know that there was a broad consensus? We may quote many learned works by highly respected scholars which say similar things giving us the impression that there was broad consensus about Stoicism. But all such accounts are largely derivative works of a smaller set of second-hand sources. We don't know how much true correspondence there is between scholarly works that we are exposed to now and what the Greek Stoics actually taught.

My view is (1) there may or may not have been many like Aristo; and (2) there may or may not have been as much consensus among the ancient Stoics as we now assume there was. So, if it is valid to assume that there was only one Aristo, and no more, it is equally valid to assume that we have no idea how much agreement there was among the early Stoics about what Stoicism was.

> 2. Most ancient Stoics did (as far as we can tell) agree that the universe is a living thing, that it has a plan and is rational.

For the reasons I outlined above, I am not that certain that 'most' ancient Stoics agreed that the universe is a living thing. I am not disputing that they might have thought that; what I am disputing is the assertion that the universe is a living thing, and that it has a plan and is rational. We already went through the reasons as to why I disagree with the statement and why you would rather suspend your judgment on that.

> 3. You can call this living universe 'God' or 'Zeus' if you like. It was probably very convenient for ancient Stoics to do so to avoid unnecessary prosecution or persecution. But we should avoid confusing this with a personal Judeo-Christian God.

I see that this is a prevalent view. But then when I read passages like this by Epictetus,

> How else could things happen with such precise regularity, if God weren't issuing orders? He orders plants to bloom and they bloom. He tells them to bear fruit and they do so... How else to explain the waxing and waning

of the moon, coming and going of the sun, and changes and fluctuations on earth?[88]

Or, like this by Seneca,

> A holy spirit dwells within us, the observer and guardian of our good and bad deeds. He treats us in the way he is treated by us. No human being is good without God; can anyone rise above fortune unless aided by him? He gives splendid and upright counsels. In every good person 'what God it is is uncertain, but a God dwells there.[89]

I cannot but wonder, in what way is this not similar to a Judeo-Christian God? Remember, Tim, I am not out to discredit Stoic physics, disprove the existence of God, challenge fatalism, or revise Stoic principles. I am only questioning the dubious connection between Stoic physics and Stoic ethics.

> 4. The SABS items don't mention God, and I think it's these views that the Stoics (or most of them) were committed to, rather than the idea of a God who sits outside of Nature.

Ancient Stoics may have used God and Nature interchangeably. But, as I pointed out in one of my earlier letters, they did attribute the qualities of what we would call God to Nature. This makes them theists. SABS items may not explicitly mention God, but they imply it.

So, I go back to my view. Because we really don't know, let's give the benefit of the doubt to Mark Vernon. Let me also agree for the time being that there was consensus among ancient Stoics, and they believed in Stoic physics and gods and determinism. I still believe that their assertion that Stoic physics was the foundation of Stoic ethics is misguided. It never was.

Towards a resolution

You say that my explanation "doesn't resolve the question of whether the ancient Stoics saw physics as foundational". I agree that we cannot resolve what the ancients thought. So, let me respond to your specific comments (in italics),

If reason rules the universe, it makes sense to understand and follow reason.

Yes, I agree. But if we assume (like I do) that we don't know what rules the universe, it still makes sense to follow reason. It is the best tool we have. No philosophy or science is possible without it. *So, why do we need a reason to follow reason?*

If everything is predetermined, it makes sense to go along with what we see as fate rather than struggle against it or try to change it.

Yes, I agree. But even if we don't believe in predetermination, it is easy enough to see that certain things are under our control and certain things are not. Once we see that, we can see the futility of struggling against what we cannot change. *So, why accept the theory of predetermination for something that is clearly observable?*

If everything is good, it makes sense to feel happy and optimistic even when apparently bad things happen.

This is very iffy. I am not sure if everything is good. We can choose to think so to cope with the world. It may even be a good heuristic. But the problem of evil –

human cruelty, child molestation, degradation of the powerless – does not go away because the Stoics say so. *So, why accept an iffy hypothesis when we can achieve the same benefit by treating it as a heuristic, whose truth value is not particularly relevant?*

> *If we really are like brothers in that we are all part of the divine, it makes sense to see ourselves as part of a large entity rather than being separate entities who should just aim for their own happiness (for example, Marcus's* Meditations *2.1).*

Yes, I agree. But our interdependency is a fact. The shirt I am wearing right now was designed in France, made in China, and sold in the U.S. It is a fact an economic downturn in the U.S. could throw many Taiwanese out of work. When someone commits suicide, it affects many other people. When Coronavirus strikes China, it is also a problem for people in other countries. Most of us don't take the time to think about these things, but our interdependency is a fact. When we reflect, I hope most of us can and do relate to the less fortunate. We do understand 'There, but for the grace of God, go I'. I daresay that many people who are civic conscious today are not so because of Stoicism. *So, why drag in divinity when humanity works just as well or better?*

> *But if we don't believe these things, why should we be Stoics rather than Epicureans or Utilitarians or Hedonists?*

We believe in Stoicism because, as I argue above, we can arrive at the same conclusions the ancient Stoics arrived at using our reason rather than obscure theories. That is my entire point. (I suspect that Stoics arrived at their conclusions using reason as well, but presented it in a shiny physics package, perhaps to make it more attractive.)

> *How would you persuade Rutherford's char that Stoicism was better than Epicureanism? Why should readers place such a high value on virtue as Stoics demand – or an even a higher one as Cynics ask? Why should we place no intrinsic value on happiness?*

This is a larger topic. So, let's explore this in a different conversation. I promise to get back to this topic later.

Oops, I got so totally involved in this, I forgot the fine port waiting for me. Let me relax with my port while I enjoy listening to your thoughts. By the way, where is my cigar?

LETTER 23. TIM TO CHUCK

 Thank you for your latest.

I feel we could go on debating the question about whether the majority of Greek Stoics thought that the physics was fundamental to their ethics and their Stoicism for a lot longer and not get much further! Perhaps we need to agree to disagree on this point.

I am torn here – I fear that further debate about this one issue would test the patience of Rutherford's char and any other readers. So, I am tempted to move on to the next part of our discussion.

But on balance I thought it would be rather rude not to reply to you on this point.

I have three reasons for continuing to believe that the physics was fundamental to most Greek Stoics. First, neither of us (certainly not me anyway!) are classicists or ancient historians. Classicists I trust, like Brad Inwood, Chris Gill, and Julia Annas think that most Greek Stoics believed in the physics and considered it fundamental (though not necessarily foundational). Unlike the case of the Emperor's New Clothes, I do not see any reason why they (Brad, Chris, and others) are motivated to be deceived about any of this.

Secondly, I think it is wrong to downplay the writings of Cicero – why should he deceive us? We know he had access to many libraries, which would have contained primary sources. I don't know the extent of the primary sources or how to interpret them. But I will grant you that Diogenes is not the most reliable secondary source and if it is the case that there are hardly any primary sources of Greek Stoicism, then perhaps caution is required about us being too certain about what they believed. But wouldn't this argument lead us to discount everything we know about Greek Stoicism? If your argument is right about the untrustworthiness of the sources, shouldn't we pretty much ignore the Greek Stoics?

But most crucially, I can glimpse at why the physics would have been fundamental.

1. If you believe in Fate, then it makes sense to go with the flow of life. If you do not, you are like the dog who chokes itself when being pulled by the cart.

2. If you believe that we humans share in the logos in terms of our rationality, then Stoic cosmopolitanism makes a lot of sense.

3. If you believe that we were made to live in communities and to be rational, then you can argue that for the virtues.

4. If you believe that the logos is providential and good, then you can accept your fate (even apparently bad things) happily, as it is all for the best, though one may not understand exactly how.

If you don't believe these things, why should you believe in virtues at all? Why should you believe that they are more important than happiness? Why should you believe in the theory of preferred indifferents?

I wonder if there is a middle ground between physics being a foundation and physics being a pedestal? One group of thinkers (including Long) believe the physics is foundational — Stoicism is "broken-backed" without the physics. There is another group of thinkers — Chris Gill and Julia Annas amongst them — who think that there is another, equally valid, way of Stoicism, supported by Cicero's *On Duties*. This is to see the physics as supporting the ethics, but not as being foundational. So, the physics isn't exactly a pedestal, but neither is it the foundation. I can see the sense in their position. I have come to think of the possibility of a 'Stoic elevator'. You can get on board the elevator with just the ethics and psychology and that will take you a long way, perhaps as far as you want to go. If you want to get off before the physics, fine. It is not, as A.A. Long suggests, a "broken-backed" Stoicism! But if you embrace the Stoic physics, then you can reap further benefits. If you believe in Providence, then you can practice *amor fati*. If you believe in pantheism, then there are more grounds for cosmopolitanism. It is instructive to compare reading Marcus Aurelius 2.1 from these two perspectives.

> *Begin the morning by saying to thyself, I shall meet with the busybody, the ungrateful, arrogant, deceitful, envious, unsocial. All these things happen to them by reason of their ignorance of what is good and evil. But I who have seen the nature of the good that it is beautiful, and of the bad that it is ugly, and the nature of him who does wrong, that it is akin to me, not [only] of the same blood or seed, but that it participates in [the same] intelligence and [the same] portion of the divinity, I can neither be injured by any of them, for no one can fix on me what is ugly, nor can I be angry with my kinsman, nor hate him. For we are made for co-operation, like feet, like hands, like eyelids, like the rows of the upper and lower teeth. To act against one another then is contrary to nature; and it is acting against one another to be vexed and to turn away.[90]*

This is my favourite Stoic quotation. Yet if you take away the Stoic physics does it not lose a good deal of its power? I am reminded of Pascal's wager[91] here. It might well pay to believe in some of the Stoic physics. What have we got to lose?

But can one make oneself believe it? And is it a good idea to do so? We may agree to disagree about some of this, and that's OK if we do. Whether we agree or disagree, we still face what for me is the key question, and one which I hope we can tackle very soon, namely – without physics, without the cobwebs, how can you justify Stoic ethics and Stoic practice?

LETTER 24. CHUCK TO TIM

 Let me start with the final few points you raised before responding to the rest.

The passage from *Meditations* you quoted can resonate with different people for different reasons. One can believe in the 'brotherhood of man' without having to subscribe to Stoic physics. One can appreciate the passage for simply putting the responsibility for our feelings on ourselves rather than others. So, if the Stoic physics aspect of the passage appeals to you the most, I have nothing against it. Neither does it necessarily contradict my belief that Stoic physics is not needed to understand and practice Stoic ethics.

Pascal's wager (the argument that it is in one's own best interest to behave as if God exists, since the possibility of eternal punishment in hell outweighs any advantage in believing otherwise) doesn't appeal to me. It seems to substitute cost-benefit analysis for rational understanding. We are trying to explore what is true, not necessarily what is beneficial. (I can see, however, why some people may gladly accept the wager, especially because it absolves us of the responsibility to think for ourselves.)

You compare two views on Stoic physics:

1. *Physics is essential.* (A.A. Long)
2a. *Physics is not essential but supportive.* (Chris Gill, Julia Annas)
2b. *Physics is a bonus.* You can do just Stoic ethics and you will be just fine. But if you can add physics to it,

you will reap greater benefits. (Your elevator analogy.)

Let me explain my position with a different analogy. Think of a cup of freshly brewed tea as Stoic ethics. Milk is Stoic physics. I like freshly brewed tea with no milk. I like the smell and the taste of the brew and I believe it is a complete drink. Then you come along and say that it is perfectly fine to drink freshly brewed tea on its own but adding milk will increase its nutritional value and add additional taste. A third friend joins us and voices the opinion that he wouldn't consider milk as optional in making tea – it is a non-negotiable part of tea.

For reasons I already discussed, I don't accept that milk is an integral part of tea, although I have no objection to anyone adding milk to theirs. The advantage in drinking tea without milk is that you can enjoy it whether you have access to milk or not, whether you like or milk or not, whether you are allergic to milk or not, whether you are a vegan or not. As far as the additional nutritional benefit of milk, I hold that it is minimal.

In summary, my view is that Stoic physics is neither necessary nor adds much value to Stoic ethics. Your (and Chris Gill's and Julia Annas') view is that Stoic physics is optional and, if pursued, can add value to Stoic ethics. The more orthodox view (held by A.A. Long and other scholars) is that Stoic ethics cannot stand on its own without Stoic physics.

Now on to the other issues you raised,

You said: Firstly, unlike the case of the Emperor's New Clothes, I do not see any reason why they (Brad, Chris, and others) are motivated to be deceived about this.

I have the utmost respect and admiration for scholars like Chris Gill and Brad Inwood and I have expressed this elsewhere in my writings. My having a different point of view does not mean that they 'were deceived' or that I am in any shape or form smarter than them. For example, no scientist (as far as I know) claims to be smarter than Einstein and yet Quantum Physics would have been abandoned if scientists had followed Einstein's rejection of it because they are not smarter than Einstein. Bill Gates famously said that "640K memory ought to be enough for anyone". Thirty years later, even the smallest toy computer is thousands of times bigger than that. I wouldn't think either Einstein or Bill Gates were motivated to be deceived. I am reluctant to subscribe to the theory that brilliant and honest people are always right. Even more interestingly, Brad Inwood himself made this observation supporting the rejection of Stoic physics,

> The narrow focus on ethical improvement is also an authentic component of ancient Stoicism.[92]

> You asked: Secondly, I think it is wrong to downplay the writings of Cicero – why should he deceive us?

Again, I wasn't downplaying Cicero or attributing any motive to him. From what I read from some scholars, Cicero has been extremely faithful to the original writings in some places but not so much in others. We all interpret what we read, and our interpretation is coloured by our knowledge, experiences, and preconceived ideas, even when we have no intention to deceive others or misinterpret what we read. Given that, if there was only one secondhand and non-contemporary account far removed in time of any philosophy, would we consider it authoritative? We don't to have reject Greek Stoicism entirely because we don't have a firsthand source and we don't have to attribute any devious motive to Cicero. But I am sure we can be skeptical of things that make less sense to us (at least to me!)

You asked: Most critically, you don't believe in [things like Fate], why should you believe in virtues at all?

For the examples you cite (dog pulled by car, cosmopolitanism, cooperating with the inevitable, et cetera), I don't see why they need the support of Stoic physics at all. They all make logical sense or logical arguments can be developed to support them. People co-operate with the inevitable (such as staying in a bad marriage because they cannot afford to divorce for economic reasons), give in to unreasonable demands because losing their job is not an option for them, etc. All such actions make logical sense to them. They don't need physics to figure these things out. Understanding that things happen as they happen and that we need to deal with what happens is 'stand-alone' wisdom and requires no support. Why things happen as they happen may be of theoretical interest but is not needed to understand Stoic ethics. Especially if the explanation is less than satisfactory.

Finally, you challenged me with this: "Why virtues and the theory of indifferents at all?"

Again, because they make psychological sense. The main rationale for Stoic virtues is that they are good for us. We don't practice them for the benefit of others because Stoicism is very clear on this point: No one can hurt or help us, and we can help or hurt no one. You don't have to accept the theory of indifferents. (The Cynics and Aristo didn't.) It is logical to reject the theory of indifferents, but it makes life easier and makes the philosophy more palatable to most people who could benefit by it. To me, the Cynics' and Aristo's stand on indifferents sounds more logical but I accept the theory of indifferents because it lets me eat my cake and have it too. It is less ascetic and calls for a less radical view of the world. But should someone reject the theory of indifferents, I would say they are probably more philosophically rigorous that I am.

LETTER 25. TIM TO CHUCK

 I really like your tea analogy. Like you, I don't like the taste of tea with all the milk, all of the traditional Stoic physics. I am probably keener than you on trying some milk with my tea – Stoicism with some of the physics. We agree that pouring all the milk into the tea spoils the brew altogether – Stoicism with all the physics is not to our taste at all.

I am also interested in going beyond personal taste and finding out which brew works for the majority of people – an analysis of Stoic week and SABS scores could help with this. Provisional analysis suggests that some of the milk (not necessarily the bits I like!) adds some value.

I think where we disagree most is in our view of the history of tea, or Stoicism. I don't see any reason to dispute the view that in olden times milk was considered an integral part of the brew.

The port bottle is nearly empty, the night is drawing in. But we still have some important issues to resolve.

In short – how would you persuade Rutherford's char that Stoicism was better than Epicureanism? Why should readers place such a high value on virtue as Stoics demand – or an even higher one as Cynics ask? Why should we place no intrinsic value on happiness?

How about Epicureanism?

LETTER 26. CHUCK TO TIM

 Let me respond to the issues you raise before the port runs out and it gets too close to sunrise. Tim, you asked me in an earlier letter,

How would you persuade Rutherford's char that Stoicism was better than Epicureanism? Why should readers place such a high value on virtue as Stoics demand – or an even a higher one as Cynics ask? Why should we place no intrinsic value on happiness?

Here is my short answer:

1. Epicureans believe that happiness can be pursued directly. Virtues are just a means of achieving it. Stoics implied that happiness cannot be pursued directly, and it is a byproduct of virtue. Current scientific evidence is more in line with the view that happiness is a byproduct: People who pursue something outside

of themselves are happier than those who pursue happiness directly.

Stoicism 1; Epicureanism 0.

2. What I consider to be the most fundamental of Stoic tenets – some things are up to us and others are not – is one of the most powerful and relatable insights. I have seen this insight bring immediate relief to many troubled people. As far as I can tell, Epicureanism has no corresponding insight. I have said in the past (more as an observation than as a conclusion) that *Stoicism is of great help to those who are troubled, Epicureanism is good for those whose life is more or less on an even keel.* We have more troubled people in the world today than ever and Stoicism is needed more than ever.

Stoicism, 2; Epicureanism, 0.

This doesn't mean that Epicureanism has no redeeming features. It does. But that would be another conversation. Briefly though, I don't have any great objection to Epicureanism, but Stoicism is somewhat more in line with my thinking and possibly with current scientific findings.

I believe I have answered all your questions to the best of my ability, meager as it may be. I know we are nervous about running out of port and losing sleep. We have to go to work tomorrow and, in your case, patients are depending on you.

We have two choices at this stage. We can stop and you can summarize our points of agreement and disagreement to wrap up the discussion thus far. You will have the final word. Or we can go for one or two more sessions while we sober up and cover two more topics: why the Stoics brought God into Stoicism in the first place and Stoic determinism as fatalism for the sake of covering the waterfront where cobwebs reside. (Is this a mixed metaphor? If it is, you can't blame me. Late nights and port tend to have that effect on me.) I leave the choice up to you.

LETTER 27. TIM TO CHUCK

 On the question "why be a Stoic rather than an Epicurean", I agree with your conclusion – be a Stoic – but for a different reason. [93]

You write,

> Epicureans believe that happiness can be pursued directly. Virtues are just a means of achieving it. Stoics implied that happiness cannot be pursued directly, and it is a byproduct of virtue. Current scientific evidence is more in line with the view that happiness is a byproduct: People who pursue something outside of themselves are happier than those who pursue happiness directly. Stoicism 1; Epicureanism 0.

I agree that people who pursue something outside of themselves are often happier than those who do not, the thing is Stoicism really tells people to not pursue happiness at all – only as a 'nice to have'. The difference is between those who are pursuing happiness every moment of the day – probably not a good mindset, those who pursue it more indirectly – "Writing to Chuck makes me happy, so I will make time for that", and not pursuing it at all.

I don't think the Epicurean spends every moment saying, "How shall I be happy in the next minute?". They are more aware of what will lead to happiness than most people, and they pursue these things – so they are like person two in my case, and Stoics like person three. So, which makes people happier?

Well, in CBT we use a procedure called behavioural activation. People keep a diary where they learn what makes them happy and gives them a sense of achievement. They then schedule more of such activities. It works. So, strategy two works.

But we also believe from Stoic Week and being Stoic for a month (SMRT) that Stoicism also leads to people being happier.[94] Is it more or less than if it were pursued more directly? We don't know, but I'd love to compare SMRT with a month of Epicureanism to find out!

I believe both roads lead to happiness. The Stoic may or may not be happier than the Epicurean. But the Stoic is getting happiness *and* a life lived well – the Epicurean gets happiness but at the expense of doing good for other people (outside of their own friendship group).

I make that Stoicism, 2; Epicureanism, 1.

You wrote,

> What I consider to be the most fundamental of Stoic tenets – some things are up to us and others are not – is one of the most powerful and relatable insights. I have seen this insight bring immediate relief to many troubled people. Epicureanism has no corresponding insight. I have said in the past (more as an observation than as a conclusion) that Stoicism is of great help to those who are

troubled, Epicureanism is good for those whose life is more or less on an even keel. We have more troubled people in the world today than ever and Stoicism is needed more than ever. Stoicism 2; Epicureanism 0.

I agree about the value of the dichotomy of control. Definitely one point for Stoicism. I disagree that Epicureanism cannot help those who are troubled. Epicurus wrote a lot about managing anxiety. Didn't Seneca borrow a lot of Epicurean ideas in his letters, for instance about facing death? So, I think the final score is, Stoicism, 3; Epicureanism, 2. Which is why I am a Stoic and not an Epicurean.

Did the Ancient Stoics *Truly* Believe in God?

LETTER 28. CHUCK TO TIM

 Thank you for your most recent letter.

I don't seriously disagree with anything you have said about Epicureanism. Let me quickly clarify a couple of things before we move on to the next topic. I didn't mean to imply that Epicureanism cannot help people. I simply said I didn't find an immediately effective and powerful statement like the dichotomy of control in Epicureanism. Neither did I mean to imply that Epicureans cannot achieve happiness. I said that the modern psychology asserts that people who pursue happiness directly are less happy than those who get involved in things outside of themselves. So, we are not that far apart after all.

Did the ancient Stoics *truly* believe in God?

As Julia Annas points out, and as discussed in in detail in Letters 10, 26, and others, Stoic ethics makes perfect sense without any extraneous mumbo jumbo. Ancient Stoics were master logicians and their propositional logic is still found useful in our digital era. It's hard to believe that they didn't figure out that Stoic ethics could function independently of Stoic physics. Maybe they didn't even truly believe in theism. As Plotinus observed,

> They [the Stoics] bring in God for the sake of appearances[95]

But why? Why did they bring in God 'for the sake of appearances'? Here I can only speculate, and I know I am treading on thin ice. So, Tim, take my speculation with a pinch of salt.

God as the answer

Dr. Wes Cecil, in his Peninsula College lectures (2019)[96], suggested that in ancient times people started with the answer 'God'. All phenomena they didn't understand, such as thunder and lightning and pestilence, they attributed to God. Even the ever-questioning Socrates didn't question the *existence* of a God, but only its version.[97]

> Socrates did not believe in the gods of the Athenians (indeed, he had said on many occasions that the gods do not lie or do other wicked things, whereas the Olympian gods of the poets and the city were quarrelsome and vindictive); Socrates

introduced new divinities (indeed, he insisted that his daimon-ion had spoken to him since childhood).[98]

Considering God as the answer is nicely illustrated in the passage below. Explaining why some things are not under our control, Epictetus says,

...the gods have placed this alone in our power, the most excellent faculty of all... the others they have not placed in our power. Was it indeed because they did not want to? I rather think, that if they could, they would have entrusted us with those also; but there is no way in which they could.[99]

Even Epicurus, who had assumed that natural phenomena can be scientifically explained, stated that gods existed,[100] even though they didn't care for humans (maybe he pretended to believe in God for his own personal safety, we will never know).

The Euclidean challenge

The first person who *didn't* offer God (or the emperor) as an explanation for natural phenomena was perhaps Euclid. His book *Elements* starts with geometric definitions and goes on to offer theorems and proofs. Euclid wasn't compelled to invoke Zeus to explain why natural phenomena are the way they are. He didn't assume that they had to be explained as God's doing. But most others around this time offered God as an explanation for natural phenomena.

Perhaps the ancient Stoics brought God in "for the sake of appearances" because they lived in a period in which God was assumed to be behind everything. Even purely logical things needed to be explained as the work of God.

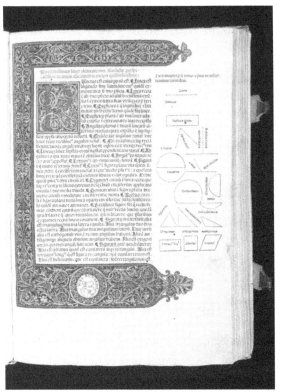

The opening page of Euclid's *Elements*.
Erhard Ratdolt (printer)

Lawrence Becker and the New Stoicism

Of all those who defend Stoic physics, Lawrence Becker stands apart. He makes a deliberate, intellectually rooted argument for revising Stoic principles, so they correspond to 'facts'. For example, Stoicism asserts that we have the absolute ability to assent appropriately even under extreme emotional stress. But what if some of the things that Stoics believe are under our control turn out to be not in our control? If the facts lead us to believe that the Stoic dichotomy argument is flawed, then, based on that, we have to modify our argument. This is clearly a valid case for creating a 'new Stoicism'.

I agree with Larry Becker that Stoic principles have to align with science. But this still doesn't make a case for Stoic physics. If, as I have argued, Stoic physics was never a true foundation of Stoic ethics, Stoicism was never derived from Stoic physics, but from a valid form of reasoning, there is no point in revising Stoic physics.

A case for empirical Stoicism

If we reject theories designed to adorn Stoicism with academic 'respectability', how do we know whether Stoic ethics needs revising? Let us start with the assumption that Stoic ethics is generally valid because many of its principles have been used in different settings (such as psychotherapeutic, combat, and catastrophic situations) and found to work. But even though it mostly works, some aspects of it may not be one hundred percent true. For example, ancient Stoics have said that we have total control over everything that is 'internal'. What if this is incorrect? What if some bodily function or chemical imbalance overrules rational judgments in some cases? Doesn't that demonstrate that we should revise Stoic physics to make it correspond to our current knowledge?

Even here, we don't need Stoic physics. After all, we aren't deriving Stoic ethics for the first time. The principles of Stoic ethics have been around for a long time. All we need to do is examine them to ensure they don't contradict the facts established by modern science. We can revise Stoicism when established science starts contradicting Stoic ethics. This is how most applied disciplines work. They don't develop their own science but use established science. I don't see any purpose in updating Stoic physics which was never the foundation of Stoic ethics as I have argued above. We may as well use currently available facts directly making it 'empirical Stoicism' as it were.

I'd like to know what you think.

LETTER 29. TIM TO CHUCK

Some more interesting thoughts about God in your last letter, Chuck. I don't think I've anything to add to what I previously said, so let's move on to determinism.

Some thoughts on updating Stoicism

Before we do, some thoughts about whether Stoicism needs updating, as Becker thinks. The Stoics were great psychologists. They may not have carried out experiments, but they *introspected* and they *observed*. How else could Seneca have written the brilliant *On Anger?* I've read the best CBT books on anger, and all I can say is that they are very similar to, but not as good as, Seneca!

Has psychology (and its applied branches such as psychotherapy and coaching) discovered anything new in the last 200 years? I believe it has, and so one of my own goals is to help integrate the two, Stoicism and modern psychology.

In the case of anger, this means encouraging contemporary psychologists to read Seneca. But in other cases, I think Stoics can usefully read psychology. For example, psychologists have developed a good understanding of the factors that perpetuate worry, depression, panic, phobias, trauma, and many specific anxiety disorders. Most of these problems exist on a spectrum, so models and techniques are relevant to many people, not just those diagnosed with a psychological disorder. For example, one consistent finding is that for low mood and depression, activity often works better than trying to change your thinking.

Stoicism-informed coaching or therapy would combine the best of both worlds, ancient and modern. Stoicism is a gem and if blended with contemporary psychology it can shine even brighter.

But this has little to do with our topic, namely Stoic physics and clearing the cobwebs. So please tell me your views on Stoicism and determinism. Cobweb or gem?

Can Compatibilism Save Stoic Determinism?

LETTER 30. CHUCK TO TIM

Before we move on to the next topic let me address your interesting point about integrating ancient Stoicism and modern psychology. I don't even think of it as integrating. I believe knowledge is unitary and the division of knowledge is arbitrary and done for the purposes of learning and understanding. Unfortunately, such divisions are taken to be real.

You raise the issue of some Stoic principles being not in line with our current experience. Let me now talk about the next major topic of Stoic physics, Stoic determinism. As an example, you cite this: "One consistent finding is that for low mood and depression, activity often works better than trying to change your thinking". How are we going to solve this issue? Are we going to refer this issue to Stoic physics and try to solve it by following wherever facts lead us? Are we going to pursue wisdom (the 'sophos' part of the word philosophy) and update what we know in light of new empirical knowledge or keep swearing allegiance to some dogma because we are committed to it?

Let me answer the question for myself. I would rather pursue knowledge than dogmas. My loyalty is not to Stoicism, but the solid wisdom on which Stoic ethics rests.

Let us now turn our attention to Stoic determinism.

Causal determinism of the Stoics

Stoics were causal determinists. After having created the cosmos, Zeus set in motion an inexorable causal chain of events. So, all events in the course of history are connected, each cause producing an effect which causes the next effect.

Who can disagree with the cause-and-effect chain? Our entire learning is based on finding causes for things that happen. Even children understand the relationship between cause and effect. But causal determinism poses a dilemma. If there is a strict causal chain from the time things were set in motion, then it can't be interrupted. Presumably, the first cause, whatever it may be, had decided the rest of history. If someone apparently interrupts it, that interruption itself has to be the effect of an earlier cause. Even though you may think that you took it upon yourself to interrupt it, you did not. You are helplessly carrying out what is in fact your part in the causal link.

The lazy argument

So, it would seem that everything is predetermined. If everything is predetermined, what need is there for us to act?[101] Why should we bother to go to a doctor when we are ill? Why should we take any responsibility for our actions? Why should we be virtuous? If we are immoral, that is predetermined. If we are not virtuous, that is predetermined too. So where is individual responsibility in all this and why should we bother to study Stoicism or any other philosophy for that matter? This argument is called the lazy argument. One may call it a 'lazy' argument, but as we will see, it is not a stupid one.

The clever argument

In an attempt to counter this 'lazy' argument, Chrysippus introduced a 'clever' argument known as *compatibilism*. It is based on the concept that there are two types of causes: *internal* and *external*.[102] [103]. The *external* cause (for example, that you fall ill) may be predetermined, but the *internal* cause (your decision to go to the doctor) is generated by you. Another person, depending on *their* personality may have decided differently. Thus, both causal determinism and your freedom/responsibility are both preserved. You are free to act, even though everything is predetermined.

To explain compatibilism, Chrysippus introduced a rather disingenuous analogy. Suppose there is a cone and a cylinder. Even if it is predetermined that both would be pushed, they don't respond the same way. When a cylinder is pushed (an *external* act) it rolls, compatible with its *internal* nature; when a cone is pushed it spins, compatible with *its* internal nature. So, although the universe (the external cause) is deterministic, the individual (the internal cause) is free to make their choice and they choose what is compatible with their nature. Magically, everything that is predetermined can be overruled and depending on what an individual decides to do (the internal cause), the course of events can be changed forever.

But wait a minute. Who determined my nature that is the cause of my internal decision? Surely, it couldn't have been me because I myself am a unit in the causal chain and my nature is a consequence of other causes. Who instilled in Donald Trump his potential responses and, in Mother Teresa, her potential responses? Who gave the cone its 'coneness' and the cylinder its 'cylinderness'? Since cones cannot choose to roll and cylinders cannot choose to spin[104], *they simply do not have a choice.* We are back to hard determinism. The apparent freedom of cones to spin and cylinders to roll is an illusion. What they could possibly do when pushed is fully determined long before they were ever pushed.[105] As Tad Brennan puts it, compatibilism is an unstable and unsatisfying compromise,

> ...the doctrine that Fate causes but Fate does not necessitate turns out to be an unstable and unsatisfying sort of compromise. [106]

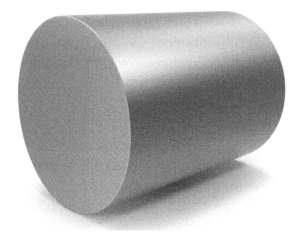

The cylinder rolls

The cone spins

The Fallacy of Reasoning by Analogy

Stoic determinism suffers from the same shortcomings as the other aspects of Stoic physics – trying to answer unanswerable questions and then trying to justify it by logical-sounding arguments that don't add up.

Can we resolve this?

Do I know the answer then? No, I do not. Can I resolve the issue? No, I cannot. I believe that this is an unresolvable issue like the existence of God. I prefer to be an agnostic on unresolvable issues. I don't want to accept *any* answer because I cannot produce the *correct* answer.

Tim, I don't really care what Stoic physics says as long as no claim is made that Stoic physics is the foundation of any substantive part of Stoic ethics. As I have said before, what anyone wants to believe is up to them, as long as I am not expected to believe it too. The foundations of Stoic ethics are logical and empirical. To claim that Stoic ethics needs the support of Stoic physics in any shape or form is a purely academic exercise and has no foundation in fact.

Belief is not evidence. Tenuous connections are not evidence. Endlessly parsing and guessing what secondary sources said is not evidence. Academic credentials are not evidence. Obscure arguments are not evidence.

Evidence, at least in my view, is what stands up to logical scrutiny and empirical observations that can be proved, disproved, or modified. And perhaps even be understood by Rutherford's char. (Actually, I like this criterion. It challenges people to make their arguments simple and understandable, and open as opposed to making them complex and pedantic.)

As I have been saying, there is no evidence whatsoever that any aspect of Stoic ethics is derived from Stoic physics. There is no evidence whatsoever to the claim that we need Stoic physics to understand Stoic ethics.

Let me conclude with these two quotes from Julia Annas:[107]

> We find no texts in which virtue, impulse, and the like are derived from Stoic physics.

> We have no support for the claim that Stoic ethics can only be understood in terms of the concepts of Stoic physics.

I couldn't have said it more explicitly. Or more unequivocally. Or more authoritatively.

LETTER 31. TIM TO CHUCK

The char speaks!

 I arrived at my office this evening to find the port bottle empty. A note was left alongside the empty bottle. I read it with not a small amount of curiosity and trepidation.

Dear Mr. LeBon

I hope you don't mind me finishing the port. I know it wasn't mine, but there wasn't much left, and anyway I thought if I finished it, it might encourage you two gents to finish your

136 • CHAKRAPANI AND LEBON

correspondence. *I'm sure it's been very interesting for you gents, but there's been a fine mess to clear up in the morning every time you've been writing, I can tell you. Speaking as a cleaner myself, how long does it take to clear up a few cobwebs?*

Mavis
(your long-suffering cleaner, and descendant of Rutherford's char)

Handling anger

Well, I have to say it was a bit of a shock. I felt a surge of anger rising up in me. "How dare she! It wasn't hers to drink! And what's all that about me creating a mess? Well, others have made a few comments but ... it's her job to clean it up for goodness sake!"

But then I remembered just in time to take a more philosophical outlook.

I pondered what had caused her to steal my port.

"Her corrupt personality!", answered my anger.

"But did she choose that personality, or did it come from her genes and upbringing?", answered the philosopher within me.

"She could still have chosen not to drink it", replied Anger.

"But this choice itself must come either from genes or upbringing or some combination of her", responded Reason. "There is no 'her' to make a choice that isn't itself determined. Blame is unfair and irrational, except perhaps for its utility."

Is Stoicism compatible with determinism?

You see, Chuck, I'm a determinist at heart. I think that libertarianism (in this sense) is incoherent, and compatibilism is hard to justify. I'm with Spinoza and Sam Harris[108] on this issue. But does it matter for Stoicism if determinism is not compatible with free will? Not a jot, I think. In fact, it increases the case for compassion – we should pity humanity for its mistakes. It also increases the need for wisdom, as Spinoza understood. The less emphasis we put on some mysterious 'will' the more we realize that we need to understand the web of causation. If I want to learn how to exercise regularly, both determinism and contemporary behavioural science tells us not to rely on willpower so much as to understand my motivation, my environment, and to manipulate it so I exercise more. The truth of determinism increases the importance of understanding and wisdom.

I forgive you, Mavis! Maybe you have a point about the cobwebs, too...

So perhaps you would like to use the next letter to add any final thoughts. Then I propose that I write a final letter summarizing where we ended up on the 'Cobwebs and Gems' ledger. I'd better keep it short, or else go out and get another bottle of port – and a new cleaner!

LETTER 32. CHUCK TO TIM

 That is a nice illustration of how anger arises in us and how we can reduce its intensity through rational analysis. And yet we are conflicted. On the one hand you 'forgive' your cleaner but, on the other hand, you want to replace her. This is how our minds oscillate between what is rational and what is emotional. Probably the ancient Stoics were aware of this too. They made the claim that only sages can act correctly under all conditions and then added that no one is a sage. I wonder what they actually meant by this: even if we act wisely most of the time, we can't expect to act wisely all the time?

Back to determinism

Moving to determinism: Determinism is, for me, another case of peeling an onion, trying to get to the core. We can stop at any point and claim that we got to the core, but there is another layer and another and another. We peel them all and we are left with nothing. As I have maintained all along, questions like God and determinism cannot possibly have definitive answers. I say this not because I know everything but because I believe that I cannot possibly know certain things because they are beyond my experience and they cannot be neatly understood by using deductive or even inductive logic. We are left with circular logic. I would rather accept that I am ignorant than use circular logic. So, I am agnostic on determinism. But, as I always maintained, I don't hold people with different views on these subjects as being necessarily wrong. I simply do not know.

Final Thoughts

LETTER 32 (CONTINUED). CHUCK TO TIM

Chuck's final thoughts

1. *Stoicism is eudemonic. Its aim is human happiness. The way to achieve it is through the practice of wisdom which consists of four 'virtues': practical wisdom, justice, moderation, and courage.*

2. *The ancient Stoics suggested that there were three aspects to Stoicism: physics, logic, and ethics. But this is open to question, as it has been since the founding of Stoicism.*

3. *We have not discussed logic in these letters. But Stoic logic covers subject matter that would not fall under what we would call logic today. While logic (as we understand the term today) is important, I don't think it really needs to be a part of Stoicism any more than it needs to be a part of any other discipline. Logic is a given.*

4. *We have discussed Stoic physics somewhat extensively. While its proponents argue vigorously that it provides the basis for Stoic ethics, no one has convincingly shown the need for Stoic physics to understand Stoic ethics. Not the*

ancient Stoics, not the modern Stoics. Stoic physics is an unnecessary distraction to understanding Stoic ethics.

5. *Stoic ethics is the gem of Stoicism and it can stand on its own. If any part of it can be shown to contradict scientific findings, we can modify that part, as and when necessary, but with great caution and care. We can go where the 'facts lead us' and not cling to the worldview that existed over two millennia ago.*

I look forward to your concluding summary of our entire discussion.

LETTER 33. TIM TO CHUCK

Tim's final thoughts

Thank you for your latest.

First things first. I didn't want to replace Mavis the char because I was angry – she quit!

I am not sure I am able to summarize the whole conversation. As well as talking about the cobwebs and gems of Stoicism, we have touched on what the Stoics really believed, determinism, God, Epicureanism, The Emperor's New Clothes, port, and Rutherford's cleaner.

We agree on much, we disagree on other things. Here are three key areas:

1. We agree that there is much practical wisdom and benefit in Stoicism based only on Ethics, without physics as support.
2. I have come to the view that physics is neither a supporting beam nor a mere pedestal. I prefer the metaphor of the 'Stoic elevator'. You maintain that it is nothing more than a pedestal.
3. In our letters, we tried to decide whether each part of the worldview was a cobweb or a gem.

	The universe in benevolent	The universe is a living thing	The universe embodies wisdom
Chuck	COBWEB Not a rational statement. Could be beneficial.	COBWEB Not a rational statement. Could be beneficial.	COBWEB Not a rational statement. True, the universe can inspire awe.
Tim	COBWEB Probably false. Not reliably helpful.	GEM Agnostic about it. Probably helpful. On balance gem.	COBWEB Not sure what it means. False in so far as I understand it.
Verdict	COBWEB 2-0	TIED 1-1	COBWEB 1-0

Thank you, Chuck, it's been most stimulating, and I hope of interest to readers too.

Notes

[1] A. A. Long, (1986) *Hellenistic Philosophy, Stoics, Epicureans, Sceptics* (Classical Life and Letters), London.

[2] Julia Annas, *Ethics in Stoic Philosophy*, in *Ancient Ethics* by Jorg Hardy and George Rudebusch, Eds.

[3] Adapted from Chuck Chakrapani, *Stoicism: My elevator pitch. Medium* (https://medium.com/stoicism-philosophy-as-a-way-of-life/stoicism-my-elevator-pitch-8ec8f7a6996b). This is a slightly modified version.

[4] For a more detailed outline of Stoic ethics from a practitioner's point of view, see https://modern-stoicism.com/how-to-be-a-stoic-when-you-dont-know-how-by-chuck-chakrapani/

[5] Julia Annas, *Ethics in Stoic Philosophy*, in *Ancient Ethics* by Jorg Hardy and George Rudebusch, Eds.

[6] Chuck Chakrapani (2018) *Stoic Minimalism.* https://modernstoicism.com/stoic-minimalism-stripping-the-dead-bark-off-orthodox-stoicism-by-chuck-chakrapani/

[7] For example, in that paper I had given reasons that *logically led me* to the conclusion that Stoic physics is not needed to understand and practice Stoic ethics. Massimo Pigliucci wrote a critique refuting my propositions with alternative arguments but without fully refuting my logic

or the reasons (see my seven propositions in Letter 20 in this book) that led me to my conclusions. When my logic is not refuted, all that means is that the critic has a contrary view on the matter, and he can support it through a different set of arguments, which is fine by me. However, as long as my logical arguments are not refuted, my conclusions based on them stand.

[8] An example: Tad Brennan (currently of Cornell University) presented a paper on Stoicism during the BMCR season several years ago. The paper contained some unorthodox views on Stoicism. As result, the entire paper was expunged from the published proceedings of the conference.

[9] Marc Tullius Cicero, His books such as *De Finibus Bonorum et Malorum, Tusculanae Quaestiones, and De Officiis.*

[10] Diogenes Laërtius, *The Lives of Eminent Philosophers.*

[11] Seneca, In general, all his Stoic works, but especially *Epistulae Morales ad Lucilium.*

[12] Epictetus, *Discourses* and *Enchiridion.*

[13] Marcus Aurelius, *Meditations.*

[14] Curtius Wachsmuth, Otto Hense (1912) Ioannis Stobaei Anthologium (3 volumes) Berlin: Weidmannsche Buchhandlung.

[15] Musonius Rufus, *Lectures* 18.

[16] Epictetus, *Discourses* 1.16.

[17] Marcus Aurelius, *Meditations* 4.21.

[18] Epictetus, *Enchiridion* 40.

[19] Musonius Rufus, *Lectures* 3, 3.

[20] See (https://modernstoicism.com/symposium-what-is-modern-stoicism/) for the debate about the nature of "Modern Stoicism". Alternative terms include "New Stoicism, "Updated Stoicism", and "Revised Stoicism". Note that some people use "Modern Stoicism" to include *anyone* interested in Stoicism in modern times, including those who wish to be as faithful as possible to all the ideas of ancient Stoics.

[21] See LeBon, T (2001) *Wise Therapy Continuum* Chapter 4 for a discussion of theories of the emotion. Modern cognitive therapists such as Beck and Ellis were inspired by Epictetus' famous line about us being affected not by events but by our interpretations of events (Epictetus, *Enchiridion 5*). For discussions about Stoicism and the cognitive theory of emotions see, for example, https://medium.com/stoicism-philosophy-as-a-way-of-life/stoic-philosophy-as-a-cognitive-behavioral-therapy-597fbeba786a and https://howtobeastoic.wordpress.com/2015/12/29/epictetus-was-right-modern-cognitive-science-supports-the-stoics-conception-of-emotions/

[22] Striker, G. (1996) "Following Nature", in: *Essays on Hellenistic Epistemology and Ethics,* Cambridge: 221 – 280.

[23] A. A. Long, (1986) *Hellenistic Philosophy, Stoics, Epicureans, Sceptics* (Classical Life andLetters), London.

[24] https://www.iep.utm.edu/stoicism/

[25] White, M.J. (2003) "Stoic natural philosophy." In: B. Inwood (ed.) *The Cambridge Companion to the Stoics.* Cambridge University Press.

[26] Brunschwig, J. (2003) "Stoic metaphysics." In: B. Inwood (ed.) *The Cambridge Companion to the Stoics.* Cambridge University Press.

[27] Algra, K. (2003) "Stoic theology." In: B. Inwood (ed.) *The Cambridge Companion to the Stoics.* Cambridge University Press.

[28] Logos is the "active reason pervading and animating the Universe". Here is another explanation of logos: "If the universe (or nature) were a computer, the logos would be its operating system, with reason being its programming language. In order to understand the universe, you have to understand that its operating system is based on reason. If you accept that nature is governed by the logos, you have to accept that everything changes, change is a constant of the universe. If you understand reason, you accept that the universe is deterministic and based on cause and effect relationships." What are Logos, Nature, and Reason in Stoicism? Stoicism (reddit.com) https://www.reddit.com/r/Stoicism/comments/6akp9s/what_are_logos_nature_and_reason_in_stoicism/ (Retrieved 23/1/21)

[29] Chuck Chakrapani, (2019) *The Stoic Atlas.* The Stoic Gym Publications.

[30] For a more detailed explanation see 'The Stoic Worldview' by John Sellars – Modern Stoicism

[31] The difference between Aristotle and the Stoics is quite subtle and not to be exaggerated. Both Aristotle and the Stoics think that the virtues should take priority over other values ("externals"). But whilst the Stoics think that virtue is sufficient for *eudaimonia,* Aristotle believes that you need a reasonable amount of externals (health,

status, friends) to flourish. I think it fair to say that most people would find Aristotle's view more in line with their intuitions.

[32]See https://modernstoicism.com/wp-content/uploads/2020/08/SABS-5.0.pdf for a description of all SABS items and how to use the SABS. For further details of the research undertaken by the Modern Stoicism team see https://modernstoicism.com/research/

[33] A.A. Long and David N. Sedley, (1987) *The Hellenistic Philosophers: Volume 1.* Cambridge University Press, UK.

[34] Brad Inwood, (2018) *Stoicism: A Very Short Introduction*, Oxford.

[35] Brad Inwood, (2018) *Stoicism: A Very Short Introduction*, Oxford.

[36] See Seligman, M. (2003) *Authentic Happiness* Nicholas Brealey, London and Frankl. V (1946) *Man's Search for Meaning* Hodder, London. See my book on positive psychology for a discussion of both Seligman's and Frankl's ideas – Lebon, T (2014) *Achieve Your Potential with Positive Psychology* Hodder, London.

[37] Zelik, M. & Gregory, S.A. (1998). *Astronomy & Astrophysics.* Sounders College Publishing Division, New York.

[38] James Lovelock, (1979) *Gaia: A New Look at Life on Earth,* Oxford.

[39] Wikipedia. *Gaia.* (Retrieved Dec. 2019)

[40] Aldous Huxley, (1945) *Perennial Philosophy,* Harper & Brothers, Publishers.

[41] I hope one day to write about Spinoza and Stoicism as there are many connections. The reader interested in

Spinoza is advised to start with Scruton, R (2202) *Spinoza: A very short introduction* OUP Oxford. For some short Modern Stoic articles on Spinoza, see, https://medium.com/stoicism-philosophy-as-a-way-of-life/spinozas-philosophical-psychotherapy-94ff758f6f15 and https://howtobeastoic.wordpress.com/2016/02/06/spinozas-stoicism/

[42] Wikipedia. *Panpsychism.*

[43] Stanford Encyclopaedia of Philosophy

[44] James Lovelock, (1979) *Gaia: A New Look at Life on Earth*, Oxford.

[45] Wikipedia. *Gaia.* (Retrieved Dec. 2019)

[46] https://www.robertlanzabiocentrism.com/are-we-part-of-a-single-living-organism/ (Retrieved Dec. 2019)

[47] Edward Fitzgerald, (1859) *The Rubaiyat of Omar Khayyam.* No. 27.

[48] https://plato.stanford.edu/entries/panpsychism/

[49] Wright, R, (2017) *Why Buddhism is True*, Simon and Schuster.

[50] John Sellars, (2018) *Hellenistic Philosophy*, Oxford.

[51] A.A. Long, (2002) *Epictetus: A Stoic and Socratic Guide to Life*, Clarendon.

[52] An 'agnostic pantheist' believes that God is immanent but not transcendent. A 'theist pantheist' believes God is both immanent *and* transcendent.

[53] Marc Tullius Cicero, *On the Nature of the Gods.*

[54] David Sedley, (2002) "The Origins of Stoic God." In *Traditions of Theology.* Ed. Dorothea Frede and Andre Laks, Brill.

[55] Epictetus, *Discourses* 1.14.

[56] Marcus Aurelius, *Meditations* 4.47 (Robin Hard's translation)

[57] Hierocles, *Ethical Fragments*, 1

[58] https://modernstoicism.com/the-debate-do-you-need-god-to-be-a-stoic/

[59] For an English version of this hymn, see https://department.monm.edu/classics/courses/clas230/Myth-Docments/cleanthes.htm

[60] A.A. Long, (2002) *Epictetus: A Stoic and Socratic Guide to Life*, Clarendon.

[61] https://modernstoicism.com/the-debate-do-you-need-god-to-be-a-stoic/

[62] https://modernstoicism.com/the-debate-do-you-need-god-to-be-a-stoic/

[63] John Sellars, (2015) "The Stoic Worldview", *Modern Stoicism*. I am not suggesting that this is necessarily Sellars' view. I am just borrowing his words.

[64] Brad Inwood, (2018) *Stoicism: A Very Short Introduction*, Oxford.

[65] Julia Annas, *Ethics in Stoic Philosophy*, in *Ancient Ethics* by Jorg Hardy and George Rudebusch, Eds.

[66] *The Internet Encyclopedia of Stoicism*, https://www.iep.utm.edu/stoicism/

[67] The sequence of letters and their contents from this letter on may not correspond to the original. We rearranged the contents and sequence of some letters, because they were discussed out of sequence and may be confusing to the reader. However, we did not change the content itself in any substantive way.

[68] Tad Brennan, (2015) "The Stoic Theory of Virtue" in *The Routledge Companion to Virtue Ethics*, Lorraine Besser-Jones and Michael Slote, eds.

[69] John Sellers, (2015) "Stoic Worldview" https://modernstoicism.com/the-stoic-worldview-by-john-sellers/

[70] Diogenes Laertius, *The Lives of Eminent Philosophers*, 7.161.

[71] Amy Richlin. *Marcus Aurelius in Love*. The University of Chicago Press, 2006.

[72] C.R. Haines. *Marcus Cornelius Fronto: Correspondence Vol. I & II.* Loeb Classical Library, 1919.

[73] Epictetus, *Fragments.*

[74] Epictetus, *Fragments.*

[75] Marcus Aurelius, *Meditations.* 9.39.

[76] Marcus Aurelius, *Meditations.* 12.14.

[77] Propositions 3 and 4 were initially a part of Letter 23.

[78] Julia Annas, *Ethics in Stoic Philosophy* in Jorg Hardy and George Rudebusch (eds.) Ancient Ethics, V&R unipress.

[79] Brad Inwood, (2018) *Stoicism: A Very Short Introduction*, Oxford.

[80] Brad Inwood, (2018) *Stoicism: A Very Short Introduction*, Oxford.

[81] Julia Annas *Ethics in Stoic Philosophy* in Jorg Hardy and George Rudebusch (eds.) *Ancient Ethics*, V&R unipress. Download available at https://www.academia.edu/9855820/Ethics_in_Stoic_Philosophy

[82] Piotr Stankiewicz, (2020) *Manual of Reformed Stoicism.* Vernon Press.

[83] Julia Annas, *Ethics in Stoic Philosophy* in Jorg Hardy and George Rudebusch (eds.) *Ancient Ethics*, V&R Unipress.

[84] Ockham's razor, *Encyclopædia Britannica*. 2010.

[85] Chuck Chakrapani, *Unshakable Freedom*, The Stoic Gym, 2016.

[86] Tim did not comment on my second proposition.

[87] We had some debate about whether to include Julia Annas' words at the start of the book. I (Tim) didn't want the reader to come away with the impression that we believe that Annas supports all our views. As I understand it, Annas' view expressed in *Ethics in Stoic Philosophy* is that physics is not necessarily foundational and yet the physics, ethics, and logic mutually support each other. I think she is right in her interpretation of the ancient Stoic and at the same time you can construct a Modern Stoicism without much of the Stoic physics. So even if the ancient Stoics thought that most of the physics were gems, Modern Stoics don't have to rely on them.

[88] Epictetus, *Discourses 1.14*.

[89] Seneca, *Letters on Morals* 41.2

[90] Marcus Aurelius, *Meditations* 2.1 transl. by George Long.

[91] Pascal's wager refers to the idea that there is less downside to believing what may not be true than not believing what may be true.

[92] Brad Inwood, (2018) *Stoicism: A Very Short Introduction*, Oxford.

[93] I (Tim) definitely don't think that Aristo or the Cynics and their theory that virtue is the only thing of value is logically superior to theory of preferred indifferents. See *Wise Therapy* for my "virtues machine" argument against virtue being the only thing of value.

[94] See https://modernstoicism.com/wp-content/uploads/2020/09/SMRT-2020-Results-1.0.pdf

[95] Enneads, 6.1.27.

[96] Wes Cecil, (2019) *History of Philosophy in Sixteen Questions* (Peninsula College Lectures).

[97] Tina Belsey and Michael Peters, (2018) *Teaching, Responsibility, and the Corruption of Youth.* Brill Sense.

[98] Stanford Encyclopaedia of Philosophy.

[99] Epictetus, *Discourses* 1.9. (Robert Dobbin, Christopher Gill), Dent 1995.

[100] Martinez, Anthony, Epicurus. *Complete works of Epicurus.* Lighthouse Books. Kindle Edition.

[101] Cicero, *On Fate*, 28.9

[102] Cicero, *On Fate* 28.9

[103] A.A. Long and David N. Sedley, (1987) *The Hellenistic Philosophers: Volume 1.* Cambridge University Press, UK.

[104] "A cylinder cannot move at will." Marcus Aurelius, *Meditations* 10.33

[105] Since I wrote this letter, I came across Tad Brennan's much more detailed challenge to compatibilism of Chrysippus. Some of Brennan's arguments are very similar to mine but framed far more elegantly (see the next endnote).

[106] Tad Brennan, (2005) *The Stoic Life: Emotions, Duties and Fate.* Oxford.

[107] Julia Annas, *Ethics in Stoic Philosophy* in Jorg Hardy and George Rudebusch (eds.) *Ancient Ethics*, V&R unipress.

[108] Sam Harris (2012) *Free Will.* Free Press.

About the Authors

Tim LeBon
Tim LeBon is the author of *Wise Therapy* and *Achieve Your Potential with Positive Psychology*. He is a philosophical life coach with a private practice in London and via Zoom. He is also an accredited CBT psychotherapist working as a senior CBT therapist in the NHS. Tim is a founding member of the Modern Stoicism team, specializing in research and assessment. His website is http://www.timlebon.com.

Chuck Chakrapani
Chuck Chakrapani is the editor of THE STOIC magazine, and author of over 15 books on Stoicism, including *Unshakable Freedom*. Chuck is a psychologist by training, a data scientist by profession, and a Stoic writer by choice. He is president of Leger Analytics, Distinguished Visiting Professor at Ryerson University, and Chief Knowledge Officer of the Blackstone Group in Chicago. You can reach him through his website TheStoicGym.com.

OTHER FREE RESOURCES FRO THE STOIC GYM

THE STOIC: A digital monthly magazine

THE STOIC, the official magazine of The Stoic Gym, is designed to bring you high-quality articles on how to live a life of happiness, serenity, and freedom using Stoic principles. By subscribing, you can have the magazine delivered to your inbox, as soon as an issue is published. *It's FREE! https://www.thestoicgym.com/the-stoic-subscribe/*

THE GOOD LIFE HANDBOOK (FREE eBOOK)

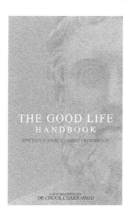

The Good Life Handbook is a modern rendition of Epictetus' classic work *Enchiridion*. The Handbook is a guide to the good life. It answers the question, "How can we be good and live free and happy, no matter what else is happening around us?"

"An inspiring read and one I plan to go back to whenever I need a little reminder that I can only control what I do, not what the world around me does." Elizabeth (Goodreads)

"This contemporary-language paraphrase of the Enchiridion *is much more accessible than other translations I have read. I was pleased to find what I was looking for - an* Enchiridion *readable enough to give to teenagers, still true to the ideas in the book."* Heather Jones

"I think this is my favorite version of the Enchiridion. *Chuck has done a fantastic job here, in my opinion."* Brendad Sonichsen

"Life-changing. Read it once, and you'll read it ten more times." Brandon Shinault

The digital edition of The Good Life Handbook is available FREE at online book stores like Amazon. https://amzn.to/2XMjpcP

A Fortunate Storm (Free eBook)

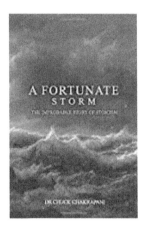

A FORTUNATE STORM Strange is the story of Stoicism. Three un-connected events – a shipwreck in Piraeus, a play in Thebes, and the banishment of a rebel in Turkey – connected three unrelated individuals to give birth to a philosophy. It was to endure two thousand years and offer hope and comfort to hundreds of thousands of people along the way. Stoicism had seven formal leaders or "scholarchs," but much of what we know of Stoicism today comes from four Stoics who lived after all the scholarchs were gone. This is the story of those eleven people. Many others contributed to Stoicism, but to make this brief and readable, Dr. Chuck Chakrapani tells the story of Stoicism through these eleven leading figures of Stoicism.

https://www.thestoicgym.com/fortunatestormfree/

Made in United States
North Haven, CT
05 November 2021

10873401R00089